APPEASEMENT IN EUROPE

**Recent Titles in
Contributions to the Study of World History**

Appeasement in Europe

A Reassessment of U.S. Policies

Edited by David F. Schmitz
and Richard D. Challener

CONTRIBUTIONS TO THE STUDY OF WORLD HISTORY, NUMBER 18

Greenwood Press
NEW YORK • WESTPORT, CONNECTICUT • LONDON

Library of Congress Cataloging-in-Publication Data

Appeasement in Europe : a reassessment of U.S. policies / edited by
David F. Schmitz and Richard D. Challener.
    p. cm. — (Contributions to the study of world history, ISSN
0885-9159 ; no. 18)
    Includes bibliographical references.
    ISBN 0-313-25925-9 (lib. bdg. : alk. paper)
    1. United States—Foreign relations—1933-1945. 2. United States—
Foreign relations—Europe. 3. Europe—Foreign relations—United
States. 4. Europe—Foreign relations—1918-1945. I. Schmitz,
David F. II. Challener, Richard D.
E806.A658   1990
327.7304—dc20   90-2941

British Library Cataloguing in Publication Data is available.

Library of Congress Catalog Card Number: 90-2941
ISBN: 0-313-25925-9
ISSN: 0885-9159

First published in 1990

Greenwood Press, 88 Post Road West, Westport, CT 06881
An imprint of Greenwood Publishing Group, Inc.

Printed in the United States of America

The paper used in this book complies with the
Permanent Paper Standard issued by the National
Information Standards Organization (Z39.48-1984).

10 9 8 7 6 5 4 3 2 1

Copyright Acknowledgments

To the students of
Whitman College

Contents

Acknowledgments

Whitman College provided various forms of financial support for this book. An Aid to Scholarship and Instructional Development Committee travel grant allowed for research at the University of Washington and Stanford University, and that same committee provided funds for typing and student research. Shirley Muse and Roberta Skiles both assisted in the typing. Teresa Dunlap compiled the bulk of the bibliography. Richard Challener got the project started. Without his encouragement I would not have taken on the task.

Introduction

David F. Schmitz

This book is designed to bring together some of the new work on appeasement policy in order to allow historians and others to examine this scholarship. There is a need to broaden the focus of research on American appeasement policy if historians are to attain a more complete understanding of that policy and what is meant when discussing the broad question of American appeasement during the 1930s. The new research addresses this need by investigating American appeasement policy toward different nations, focusing on the ideology of policymakers and the influences of different groups on the development of an appeasement policy by the Franklin Roosevelt administration, asking new questions concerning the role of antibolshevism, and examining appeasement as part of a larger quest for stability in Europe during the 1930s.[1]

Over the past twenty-five years the study of American appeasement has focused primarily on U.S.–German relations.[2] However, by addressing the question of appeasement outside of bilateral U.S.–German relations, and the resulting preoccupation with geopolitical explanations, the essays presented here raise new questions and provide different and illuminating insights concerning not only appeasement but the nature of American foreign policy prior to World War II. Moreover, by deepening our knowledge of American appeasement policy, this new scholarship brings us closer to a more complete understanding of how the United States responded to the broad challenge posed by the rise of fascism in Europe during the 1930s.

Until the early 1960s, the study of Roosevelt's diplomacy and the coming of World War II focused on the debate between the Roosevelt "internationalists," who argued that the Axis challenge drew the United States into the war in defense of American interests, and the Roosevelt "revisionists," who argued that the president manipulated an isolationist nation into that war.[3] As previously classified materials and the personal papers of policymakers became available, however, many scholars challenged the old interpretation of American isolationism. Scholars began to investigate the actual policies pursued by the Roosevelt administration. Among the most important questions raised was whether American policy toward Adolf Hitler was one of appeasement. If so, how do we define appeasement and what was the nature of that policy?

Most historians agree that the word appeasement was often used by American policymakers to describe their attempt to reach a peaceful, negotiated accommodation with Fascist Italy and Nazi Germany. During the 1930s, the term did not carry the negative and emotional connotations that it has carried since that time. By appeasement, American officials meant a policy that sought to prevent German and Italian aggression by applying either economic pressure or providing those nations with incentives for cooperation with the Western democracies. Public opposition to American involvement in European affairs surely hampered the Roosevelt administration in formulating a precise, consistent response to the growing crisis in Europe. Yet it was exactly this restraint that made the pursuit of appeasement so attractive to many upper-level officials in the State Department. Appeasement allowed them to follow a policy that sought to ease the danger of war in Europe without committing the United States to any collective security agreements or direct involvement in European politics.

There is also a general agreement that American appeasement policy was different from that of Great Britain. The United States believed that economic adjustments leading to a general settlement of all of Europe's problems had to be the first steps taken in dealing with Germany and Italy. Britain, on the other hand, followed a policy of piecemeal readjustments of the (Treaty of) Versailles order—particularly political and territorial agreements—before a general settlement could be reached. At this point, however, the agreement among historians concerning appeasement breaks down. The questions of why the United States pursued an appeasement policy, why it was different from that of Great Britain, and what its ultimate objectives were deeply divide those who have studied this issue. Within this context, three distinct schools of interpretation have emerged to explain this policy.

The first full account of United States appeasement was Arnold Offner's *American Appeasement* published in 1969. It remains the most detailed study of American appeasement policy and Nazi Germany. Geo-political questions and the influence of isolationism set the parameters for Offner's investigation. He argued that American leaders adopted a policy of appeasement in order to redress German grievances with the Versailles treaty, many of which they saw as justified. They did this, however, unaware of or blind to the true nature of the threat that Nazi Germany presented. Appeasement, therefore, was a shortsighted policy developed by American leaders to try to prevent the outbreak of war in Europe.[4] In later writing, Offner is more precise about what he means by appeasement, arguing that American policymakers believed that through arms limitation, access to raw materials and markets, and reduced trade barriers, "political appeasement in Europe could be achieved through economic appeasement."[5] But for Offner, American policymakers saw the German threat too late, and they defined that threat in military and political terms, not economic.

German historians, most notably Hans-Jurgen Schröder, have argued that American economic appeasement was a policy designed to place pressure on Germany to deal with a challenge that was primarily economic. Further developing points originally put forward by William Appleman Williams,[6] Schröder argues that from 1934 to 1939 the United States became locked into an economic battle with Nazi Germany. In order to tame Germany and protect its liberal international ideology (the Open Door) and multilateral trade policies under the Reciprocal Trade Agreement program, the Roosevelt administration offered economic arrangements that would steer Germany away from economic autarchy and bilateral trade policies. This would ensure both an American-led international economy and a peaceful solution to Germany's problems. But Germany's refusal to follow Washington's lead brought about conflict. It was this clash, particularly in Latin America and the Balkans, that ultimately led to American opposition to Germany and involvement in World War II. Economic appeasement was, therefore, a policy designed to bring American economic power to bear on Germany to prevent it from expanding its autarchic economic policies and to make German leaders realize the futility of their efforts.

Patrick Hearden has most recently published a full analysis of Roosevelt's policy building upon this interpretation. In his book *Roosevelt Confronts Hitler*, Hearden argues that "American leaders were primarily concerned about the menace that a triumphant Germany would present to the free enterprise system in the United States."[7] In his analysis he goes beyond Schröder in arguing that the Roosevelt administration sought to prevent the outbreak of general European war because it feared, Roosevelt and Under Secretary of State Sumner Welles in particular, not only that Germany might win but that another long European war would lead to revolutionary conditions and the possible triumph of communism on much of the continent. He concludes, therefore, that Roosevelt sought to provide the carrot of economic appeasement to persuade Germany to cooperate with the Western democracies while at the same time wielding the stick of the threat of American military opposition.

Finally, C. A. MacDonald, in *The United States, Britain and Appeasement, 1936–1939*, argues that American appeasement policy was part of an overall effort to establish the Open Door as the basis for European peace. Unlike Schröder, MacDonald sees the Open Door policy as leading to efforts to accommodate Nazi

Germany, not confront it. He emphasizes the role played by German "moderates" in American policymakers' thinking prior to 1938 in order to explain Washington's policy. It was believed that these "moderates"—industrialists, bankers, and Nazi officials such as Hermann Goering—supported U.S. efforts to establish an Open Door system in Europe. American policy was designed, therefore, to aid the position of these groups within Germany by easing the economic crisis which had led Germany to its misguided adoption of autarchy and expansion. Economic appeasement was seen as the alternative to "an expanding totalitarian system led by German and Japanese 'extremists' which would exclude the United States from world markets and undermine its position in Latin America."[8]

While all of these studies have greatly enhanced our understanding of Roosevelt's foreign policy and his administration's response to Hitler's Germany, no consensus interpretation has emerged. Moreover, although MacDonald's study examines both American and British policies, these works all leave important areas unexplained and other questions unanswered. Schröder correctly focuses on the economic policy differences between the United States and Germany, particularly concerning Latin America, yet he overlooks the efforts at accommodation that Offner and MacDonald document. In addition, as MacDonald demonstrates, economic warfare was not the only policy alternative for dealing with German autarchy. On the other hand, Offner divides politics and economics in a manner that would have been unrecognizable to Secretary of State Cordell Hull and other senior State Department officials. Furthermore, Offner does not investigate what policymakers thought about fascism, how they understood its growth, and how that view influenced an appeasement policy being developed in the midst of the Great Depression. Although political challenges seemingly confronted the Western democracies from both the right with Nazi Germany and Fascist Italy and the left with the Spanish and French Popular Front movements and the Soviet Union, the dimension of ideology is surprisingly addressed only in Hearden's work. Finally, Hearden curiously excludes strategic and national security considerations from his analysis of the coming of war. It appears that after 1938, economic, strategic, and political reasons all called for opposition to Nazi Germany.

The chapters presented here begin in part to resolve some of these disagreements. But by examining new geographic areas and issues, they raise new questions and problems. The ideological dimensions of appeasement have long been overlooked by historians. Douglas Little's work on the British and American response to the Spanish Civil War addresses the problem of how to contain the right without aiding Soviet foreign policy. Little has extended the analysis developed in his book *Malevolent Neutrality*, which covered the years 1931–36, to include the years 1936–39. Anglo-American nonintervention policies, he argues, did not stem primarily from a desire to buy badly needed time for rearmament and collective security, but rather from a desire to contain alleged Bolshevik subversion in Western Europe. The State Department and the Foreign Office had worried about bolshevism in Spain since the inception of the republic in 1931. British and American policymakers, therefore, regarded a Franco triumph as a more attractive alternative than the continuation of Spain's Popular Front government.

Little's analysis sheds new light on American embargo policies that deprived the Republican government of badly needed arms and munitions and on the influence of antibolshevism on American policy. On the latter point, Little and Schmitz agree that this influence was important and offer evidence that the appeasement policy toward Germany was also framed within a State Department dominated by an anti-Communist ideology. As Little notes, "through the spring of 1938 U.S. policy remained firmly in the hands of State Department anti-communists." In addition, his comments that Roosevelt desired to draw Mussolini away from Hitler also support much of Schmitz's argument. Together these interpretations call for a closer examination of the ideology of American policymakers and its influence on the shaping of the Roosevelt administration's European policy.

Previous work on American appeasement has also failed to fully investigate the influence of the prior American experience with

Fascist Italy on policy toward Nazi Germany and the attempts to use Mussolini as a moderating force on Hitler. As Schmitz's work on American policy toward Mussolini's regime demonstrates, American policymakers formed their initial analysis and policy toward Nazi Germany out of their experience with, and in comparison to, Fascist Italy. In particular, the key analysis of a "moderate"/"extremist" split was one that was first applied to the Fascist party in Italy.[9] Moreover, American experience with Mussolini led policymakers to the conclusion that Il Duce could be a moderating influence on Hitler. The Italo-Ethiopian war only brought a temporary halt to these views and did not lead to the development of an anti-Fascist policy. American experience with Italy, therefore, is important for understanding why American officials believed appeasement would work and how they expected to implement that policy.

Little, and Schmitz to a lesser extent, find key State Department officials, such as Under Secretary of State Welles, European Division Chief J. Pierrepont Moffat, James Dunn, and William Phillips, wielded great influence in the shaping of American policy. In addition, American desires to cooperate with Great Britain influenced policy toward Spain and Italy. Richard Harrison and Jane Karoline Vieth, however, find this cooperation more difficult in direct U.S.–Great Britain relations. Harrison sees Roosevelt dominating policy with Great Britain and both find substantial areas of disagreement that prevented the development of a consistent joint American-British policy.

The question of Roosevelt's response to British appeasement is crucial for understanding American policy. Roosevelt clearly was not opposed to legitimate and peaceful appeasement by Britain. The British, Harrison points out, had to take the lead in response to the German threat, and Roosevelt attempted to encourage them and assure them of American support short of war. But the president feared what he saw as "irresponsible" appeasement and sought to prevent the British from reaching bilateral arrangements with Germany that appeared to be peace at any price. For the United States, appeasement had to be a redressing of Germany's

legitimate grievances within an overall European settlement, not
the submission to extravagant German demands that would not
prevent conflict but help bring it about.[10] So while Roosevelt
sought a "partnership with Great Britain" that was the "central
object of FDR's foreign policy and crucial to his goals in the
world," he was unable to convince Neville Chamberlain of the
wisdom of his vision and gain his support in forging a united policy
against the dictators.

Given Harrison's detailed description of Chamberlain's distrust
of the United States and Roosevelt, and the sense in London that
it was still a British world and that European affairs were primarily
a British concern, it is not difficult to see why Great Britain did not
want to rely upon the United States. The Versailles treaty and the
London Economic Conference of 1933, to take just two examples,
served to confirm such a view. In a very different manner, Harrison
arrived at similar conclusions to MacDonald's on this point. Yet
why then did Chamberlain take American Ambassador to Great
Britain Joseph P. Kennedy into his confidence? This is the subject
of Vieth's essay.

Vieth reexamines the crucial events leading up to the Munich
agreement and its aftermath through a study of the thoughts and
actions of Chamberlain, Roosevelt, and Kennedy, and their critics,
such as Anthony Eden. Her work, particularly concerning the role
of Ambassador Kennedy, raises significant questions and offers
new explanations for the agreement and its impact. The support
Kennedy provided Chamberlain indicates that there was ground
for greater cooperation between the United States and Great Britain
prior to 1938 only if the United States accepted a subordinate status
and the goals of British policy. What is not discussed were the other
problems which hampered British-American relations, such as
American free trade policies and British desires to hold onto its
dominant economic position in parts of the world that led to
conflicts between Washington and London early in the decade and
were not fully overcome even with the threat of war.

While readers will draw their own conclusions and ideas from
reading these chapters, this book contains a unique feature in the

form of a critique by Wayne S. Cole. This has been included in order to help place the contributions within the literature and to stimulate thought. His comments are based upon a reading of the final chapters and the authors have not been asked to respond to his comments.

In addition to the points raised in Cole's essay, some other general themes emerge from the collection. First, the role of ideology in shaping American policy toward the difficult problems of Europe needs further investigation, particularly concerning the most prominent State Department officials who developed and opposed U.S. appeasement policy. How did they understand the development of German economic autarchy and revisionism? Why did they believe that autarchy would drive Germany to economic chaos and military expansion?

It is clear that there was a split within the State Department between appeasers and anti-appeasers. Appeasers, such as J. Pierrepont Moffat and James Dunn, were officials who rejected a collective security system directed against Germany, feared long-term instability would lead to the spread of bolshevism, and believed that many of Germany's demands were legitimate. They argued, therefore, that the United States should seek an accommodation with Fascist Italy and Nazi Germany, regardless of their internal policies, in order to remedy the Germany problem, restore stability to Europe, and avoid a disastrous war. Anti-appeasers, such as Assistant Secretary of State George Messersmith, argued that German expansion was the central problem in Europe and had to be met with collective security arrangements and economic pressure. Indeed, they argued that economic pressure should be used on Germany in order to create as much economic strain on the Third Reich as possible in the hope that this might lead to an overthrow of the government by more moderate elements. Why the appeasers were able to dominate policy until at least 1938 requires more study into the working of the State Department at this time.

Was there an absence of a coherent American policy? Sumner Welles twice offered overarching schemes for a settlement of Europe's problems. These were defeated not because of isolationism or domestic opposition, but due to British rejection. Did Roosevelt's hesitancy, and the failure of the implementation of a full appeasement policy, therefore, owe more to his inability to find common ground with Great Britain? As this book demonstrates, the United States was able to carry forward a consistent policy toward Spain and Italy when it generally supported the lines of British policy.

Finally, this combined scholarship demonstrates that it is necessary for American policy to be studied toward all of Europe, including the Soviet Union, for a complete understanding of American appeasement. President Roosevelt—despite the difficulties his actions pose to historians and their particular interpretations—and his senior advisors saw the problems of Europe as interrelated. A universal solution, with the problem of Germany at the center, was desired. The chapters that follow represent a part of this continuing investigation.

NOTES

1. For examples of this work see David F. Schmitz, *The United States and Fascist Italy, 1922-1940* (Chapel Hill: University of North Carolina Press, 1988); Douglas Little, *Malevolent Neutrality: The United States, Great Britain, and the Origins of the Spanish Civil War* (Ithaca, N.Y.: Cornell University Press, 1985); Richard A. Harrison, "Appeasement and Isolation: The Relationship of British and American Foreign Policies, 1935-1938" (Ph.D. diss., Princeton University, 1974); Jesse H. Stiller, *George S. Messersmith: Diplomat of Democracy* (Chapel Hill: University of North Carolina Press, 1987); Frederick W. Marks III, "Six Between Roosevelt and Hitler: America's Role in the Appeasement of Nazi Germany," *Historical Journal* (December 1985); Jane Karoline Vieth, "Joseph P. Kennedy and British Appeasement: The Diplomacy of a Boston Irishman," in Kenneth P. Jones, ed., *U.S. Diplomats in Europe, 1919-1941* (Santa Barbara, Calif.: ABC-Clio, 1981).

2. The most important works on American appeasement policy, all of which are discussed below, are Arnold Offner, *American Appeasement: United States Foreign Policy and Germany, 1933-1938* (New York: W. W. Norton, 1969); Hans-Jurgen Schröder, *Deutschland und die Vereinigten Staaten 1933-1939* (Weisbaden, West Germany: F. Steiner, 1970); Patrick Hearden, *Roosevelt Confronts Hitler: America's Entry into World War II* (DeKalb: Northern Illinois

University Press, 1987); C. A. MacDonald, *The United States, Britain and Appeasement, 1936–1939* (New York: St. Martin's Press, 1981). See also Offner's, Schröder's, and MacDonald's chapters in Wolfgang J. Mommsen and Lothar Kettenacker, eds., *The Fascist Challenge and the Policy of Appeasement* (London: George Allen & Unwin, 1983) for useful summaries of their arguments.

3. For excellent overviews of this literature, see Wayne S. Cole, "American Entry into World War II: A Historiographical Appraisal," *Mississippi Valley Historical Review* 43 (March 1957); Robert A. Divine, ed., *Causes and Consequences of World War II* (Chicago, Ill.: Quadrangle Books, 1969), pp. 3–44; and Justus D. Doenecke, "Beyond Polemics: An Historiographic Re-Appraisal of American Entry into World War II," *History Teacher* 12, no. 2 (1979): 217–51. The terms Roosevelt "internationalists" and "revisionists" are Cole's.

4. Offner, *American Appeasement*, pp. 275–80.

5. Offner, "Appeasement Revisited: The United States, Great Britain and Germany, 1933–1940," *Journal of American History* 64 (September 1977): 363–93; and "The United States and National Socialist Germany," in Mommsen and Kettenacker, eds., *Fascist Challenge and the Policy of Appeasement*, quote p. 418.

6. William Appleman Williams, *The Tragedy of American Diplomacy* (New York: Dell Publishing Co., 1962), pp. 162–201.

7. Hearden, *Roosevelt Confronts Hitler*, p. x.

8. MacDonald, *United States, Britain and Appeasement*, p. x.

9. Schmitz, *United States and Fascist Italy*, pp. 60–84, 140–41.

10. See also David Reynolds, *The Creation of the Anglo-American Alliance 1937–1941* (Chapel Hill: University of North Carolina Press, 1982).

APPEASEMENT IN EUROPE

1

American Appeasement

Wayne S. Cole

"The United States opposed . . . ." "Americans believed . . . ."
"The administration took the position that . . . ." "The Department
of State tried to . . . ." "The White House gave its approval to . . . ."
Such collective nouns perform useful functions in verbal expres-
sion. All may be correct—in a sense; all usually are wrong—to a
degree. And all illustrate the difficulty of trying to discover,
describe, explain, and evaluate the roles of the United States, its
leaders, and its people in the history of appeasement in the 1930s.

During that decade the United States included more than 130
million people, and they embraced every imaginable point of view
on foreign affairs. Even with the help of polling techniques, it was
difficult to determine what foreign policies "the people" favored
or opposed. Similarly, their elected representatives in Congress
rarely united on anything in foreign affairs. Those who served on
the powerful Senate Foreign Relations Committee nearly always
included a dissenting minority on any specific foreign policy issue.
Legislators knew that the powers of Congress in foreign affairs
were limited, largely negative, and that under the Constitution the
president had all executive powers in foreign affairs. But that did
not prevent them from speaking out on behalf of or in opposition
to any conceivable policy in foreign affairs.

Under the secretary of state (Cordell Hull, most of the decade),

State Department officials and foreign service officers provided information and guidance on foreign affairs; they tried to implement policies decided by their superiors. The federal bureaucracy was tiny in comparison with today, but even then agreement was rare on any foreign policy issue. Its individual officers normally obeyed orders on policy matters, but personal values intruded as well.

The president (charismatic Franklin D. Roosevelt from 1933 until his death on April 12, 1945) under the Constitution was the official spokesman for the United States in foreign affairs. But even the president's powers were not absolute or unlimited. They were defined in the Constitution and variously shared with Congress. Members of the president's White House staff did not speak with a single voice; his advisers interpreted the president's wishes on foreign affairs with varied nuances. Even Roosevelt himself could use different language and different emphases in conversations, speeches, letters, and other communications at different times in different circumstances.

All that diversity underscores both the ease of advancing different (even conflicting) generalizations on the history of American foreign affairs, and the difficulty of defining precisely what the United States, its government, and its people did and did not believe and do relative to appeasement in Europe in the 1930s. Diversity and exceptions were the rule.

And then there is the term appeasement itself. Scientists and social scientists may invent precise technical terms to identify elements or processes they discover or develop. Historians do not have that privilege. They are stuck with terms created and used by others in the past, and it is to usage in the past that they must turn in trying to define those terms or concepts. Unfortunately, historical usage was rarely neat, precise, and uniform; many different people in many different circumstances used specific terms (such as "appeasement") in many different ways. In recreating, understanding, and explaining the past the historian must use those terms, not according to some dictionary definition or individual preference, but rather according to the myriad ways those terms were used and applied in the past.

Even values attached to terms may change over time. In the mid-1930s many used the term appeasement to describe policies in which they placed high hopes and enlightened value. In time, more used it as a pejorative term to discredit both its advocates and its consequences.

It is difficult to find precise historical definitions of "appeasement."[1] It was as much an attitude of mind as a specific policy. Appeasement was not a synonym for diplomacy, negotiation, compromise, or even necessarily for efforts to prevent war and preserve peace—though all those could be parts of the appeasement process.

To a substantial degree appeasement was a product of World War I and its aftermath. It operated from the assumption that the Versailles treaty and other treaties ending World War I were, to some degree, unjust, unfair, and unwise. The victors had not treated the defeated (and some of the victorious) states properly. The difficulties and crises between the wars grew out of efforts by "wronged" peoples and states to right the wrongs inflicted on them at the close of the war. If the injustices of the Versailles treaty were corrected, states and people could become less restless and more content. The dangers of war could be reduced or eliminated.

Appeasement also grew out of the fear of war. World War I, the Great War, had destroyed millions of Europe's finest young men, shattered the economies of European states and their people, strained the political institutions of every country, and radically dislocated older security arrangements. Any person of a later generation who can react to those horribly destructive realities of World War I in casual, detached, intellectualized, or "ho hum" terms simply lacks the empathy and compassion essential for properly thinking, writing, or speaking on the subject. Given scientific and technical developments of the times, everyone assumed that a second world war would be immeasurably more horrible and destructive than the first had been. Later generations who had never experienced the horrors of World War I could lightly ridicule the cowardice that such fears manifested. But such ridicule brings no credit to the quality of empathy or compassion of those critics—whatever conclusions one ought to draw for international affairs in the 1930s.

In all of that, appeasement was an active, not a passive, approach to international affairs. It required action. Neville Chamberlain did not sit back and do nothing; he saw a responsibility to take diplomatic initiatives to preserve peace and prevent war. Chamberlain went to Hitler, not the other way around.[2]

During most of its independent history the United States had not played positive, active roles in trying to influence diplomatic, political, military, and security policies in Europe. And most Americans continued to oppose involvement in European affairs in the 1930s.[3] Appeasement was largely a product of reasoning by leaders of European countries—particularly by foreign policy leaders in Great Britain and France. British Prime Minister Neville Chamberlain was the central figure in the history of appeasement in Europe in the 1930s. Chamberlain neither sought, expected, nor greatly valued active input by the United States in shaping or implementing those appeasement policies. In Chamberlain's view it was "always best and safest to count on nothing from the Americans but words."[4] To a striking degree appeasement in Europe grew out of the assumption that the United States would not play a substantial role in European security matters. The history of appeasement in the 1930s is primarily a European subject in which the United States and its leaders played only marginal roles.

Given the fuzziness and diversity of definitions of appeasement, it can be extremely difficult to identify when, how, or even if the United States pursued appeasement policies in Europe in the 1930s. In his 1940 campaign for election to a third term as president, Roosevelt effectively discredited his isolationist or non-interventionist opponents by calling them "appeasers."[5] Americans and their leaders rarely used the term appeasement to describe United States foreign policy. The variety of emphases and interpretations advanced by the several contributors to this book can be justified and explained by the varied, ambiguous, and even contradictory character of the subject on which they have focused their scholarly attention.

Possibly the best chapter in this volume may be "The United States and Great Britain: Presidential Diplomacy and Alternatives to Appeasement in the 1930s," by Richard A. Harrison. Harrison based his chapter on extensive research in archival and manuscript sources both in Great Britain and in the United States, as well as in published primary and scholarly secondary accounts from the United States, England, and various European states. He immersed himself in his subject, allowing his perspectives to develop and mature. He wrote clearly and boldly. To simplify his task, Harrison focused largely on the values and actions of only one person, President Roosevelt. The result is urbane, well-structured, and thought-provoking.

Harrison advanced a clear thesis and developed it consistently throughout his chapter. He wrote: "Partnership with Great Britain was the central objective of FDR's foreign policy and was crucial to his goals in the world." He contended that "Roosevelt's approach to Britain was fundamentally antagonistic to what appeasement had become by 1935."

As Harrison saw it, "London's refusal to recognize and respond to Roosevelt's overtures was the single most important reason his initiatives failed." Domestic influences within the United States also added to the president's difficulties. Despite his values, according to Harrison, Roosevelt "was constrained by the anti-European, unilateralist sentiment called isolationism, greatly strengthened in the 1930s by revisionist criticism of American involvement in the World War and by the Great Depression." According to Harrison, "Roosevelt opposed isolationism and appeasement because both left the initiative in world affairs to governments that were prepared to destroy the international order to get what they wanted. Yet he could not challenge isolationism directly. He intended to 'educate' the American people gradually." Chamberlain cynically expected and planned on little help from the United States or Roosevelt. His attitude provided little for the American president to work with on the far side of the Atlantic.

Anthony Eden and Winston Churchill hopefully envisaged and worked for a larger, more constructive role by the United States in European affairs. But Eden resigned his post as foreign minister early in 1938, and Churchill did not become prime minister until 1940 after the failure of appeasement was apparent to all. Harrison carefully traced, issue by issue, year by year, Roosevelt's persistent efforts to make his views known and America's weight felt in European peace and security concerns. Harrison made clear the feebleness of those efforts individually, their inadequacy from British perspectives, and the lack of receptiveness and encouragement that the president's initiatives won from Chamberlain's government. It was not surprising that Roosevelt's frustrations led him to exclaim that no one in Europe cared "a continental damn about what the United States thinks or does." Similarly, Chamberlain vented his cynicism by exclaiming in 1938 that "the Americans are so rotten . . . it does not matter . . . who we send" to serve as ambassador to the United States. The frustrations and disappointments on one side fed on the frustrations and discouragements on the other; each was impatient with the timidness and caution of the other.

With the failure of appeasement in Europe, with the explosion of terrifying Nazi aggression and war, with the fall of Chamberlain and the rise of Churchill and Eden in 1940, with the increasingly bold leadership by Roosevelt in the face of Axis aggression abroad and eroding isolationist strength at home, those frustrations declined. Hope replaced cynicism, and boldness increasingly replaced timidness as the United States under FDR and Great Britain under Churchill drew closer together in opposition to the Axis challenges. The result was war, a terrible war. But the result was also victory over Hitler and the Axis powers, and renewed hope for Western security, world peace, and democracy and freedom.

As Harrison concluded, FDR's "policy toward Great Britain was always based upon the need for a British posture to whose support he could rally the United States," and "British appeasement made his task incalculably more difficult." Harrison recognized that "the president's confidential overtures did not of themselves constitute an effective foreign policy," but "because of Roosevelt there was an alternative available to appeasement." Because of Chamberlain "it was never fully explored." Harrison's treatment of Roosevelt's actual performance at the time of the Munich conference is skimpy. But his analysis of Roosevelt's perspectives on foreign affairs in the 1930s is wholly consistent with my own findings in the course of some forty years of research and writing on the history of American foreign relations in the Roosevelt years.[6] My only substantial reservation or caveat is one of degree or tone. Harrison stripped away the thick underbrush and left the president's views and efforts clearly and sharply exposed; he advanced his interpretation clearly and boldly as he should have. Nonetheless, that very clarity and boldness may distort the reality.

Roosevelt often was uncertain just what actions he might take, what methods he might use, that could win British cooperation and could prove effective in Europe. It was characteristic of the president's tone when, in March 1936, he wrote to Ambassador William E. Dodd in Berlin, "If in the days to come the absolutely unpredictable events should by chance get to the point where a gesture, an offer or a formal statement by me would, in your judgment, make for peace, be sure to send me immediate word. But the peace must be not only peace with justice but the kind of peace which will endure without threat for more than a week or two."[7] His thoughts and actions were more hesitant, cautious, tentative, exploratory, and less doctrinaire than one might conclude from reading Harrison's chapter.[8] Harrison knew about all that secrecy, deviousness, obscurity, and even hesitancy—but he swept much of it away so readers could more clearly see and understand what the president was trying to do and how. In the process of clarifying central realities of FDR's attitudes and efforts toward Europe in the 1930s, however, Harrison provided an overall portrait that, in its very clarity, may distort the image one might have obtained at the time.

Harrison's chapter provides a solid framework from which to view and evaluate the other analyses advanced in this book, including Jane Karoline Vieth's chapter on "Munich and American Appeasement." That title is somewhat misleading. The chapter actually focused on the values, role, and significance of Joseph P. Kennedy's service as United States ambassador to Great Britain, particularly before, during, and after the Munich conference. In Vieth's words, Kennedy's "position was set and remained constant until the outbreak of war: support the appeasement policy for Britain and maintain American isolation." The chapter portrays Kennedy as the archetypical American appeaser who approved, encouraged, reinforced, and applauded Chamberlain's appeasement policies. It also points to the internal contradiction between Kennedy's appeasement activities on the one hand and his isolationism on the other.

Ambassador Kennedy's performance was hardly what President Roosevelt had expected of that Irish-American Catholic, and surely it was not what the president wanted. As Britain turned away from appeasement in 1939–40, and as Roosevelt and his government moved more boldly to help Britain against Nazi Germany, Kennedy fell from favor both in Britain and in the United States. At the same time, beginning in the early autumn of 1939, direct secret personal communication between Roosevelt and Churchill essentially displaced both Kennedy in London and Lothian and Halifax in Washington as communication conduits between the two leaders. Kennedy's departure from government service at the end of 1940 was wholly consistent with the abandonment of appeasement in England and with the erosion of isolationist strength in the United States. Roosevelt and Churchill prevailed; Chamberlain and Kennedy—and Hitler—did not.[9]

Vieth's chapter was based on less extensive research in original sources than were the chapters by Harrison, Schmitz, and Little. It added little to available knowledge on either American appeasement in general or on Kennedy's role in particular. It contained no surprises that might force fresh thinking on the subject. Nonetheless, it is factually accurate and analytically sound. And it is consistent with the solid interpretive framework provided by Harrison. The principal question that Vieth (and Harrison) left unan-

swered concerning Kennedy may be why (if Roosevelt attached
such great importance to Anglo-American accord) FDR appointed
Kennedy to that important diplomatic post in the first place.
And why did he not replace him sooner than he did? The explanation
may have been simple politics. Roosevelt was rewarding a wealthy
and generous long-term political supporter. And he did not wish
to alienate the large Irish-American and Catholic voting population by
dismissing him. Conceivably he did not fully anticipate Kennedy's
warm identification with Chamberlain's appeasement policies (and
with American isolationism later). Although he valued close relations with Great Britain, Roosevelt felt no special kinship with
Chamberlain and his policies, so the quality of the representative
to that particular government may not have seemed so vital as it
might have to a government with different perspectives. Roosevelt
had no shortage of personal links with leadership circles in Britain.
And the developing correspondence between FDR and Churchill
from 1939 onward made the ambassadorial posts both in London
and in Washington less vital than they might have been otherwise.
None of the three men who served as United States ambassadors to
Great Britain while Roosevelt was president (Robert W. Bingham,
Joseph P. Kennedy, and John G. Winant) was a diplomatic heavy-
weight. Roosevelt did not rely heavily on any of them for guidance
or delicate diplomatic matters. Nonetheless, Vieth's treatments of
Kennedy, Chamberlain, Roosevelt, and appeasement are consistent with and reinforce the broader and more solidly researched
images provided in Harrison's chapter.

David F. Schmitz's chapter on " 'Speaking the Same Language':
The U.S. Response to the Italo-Ethiopian War and the Origins of
American Appeasement" provides additional insights and raises
further questions on the subject. Focusing on one particular tree
may make it impossible to see the whole forest. Likewise, concentration on the Czechoslovakian crisis and its temporary resolution
at the Munich conference is proper, as is detailed examination of
Chamberlain's personal negotiations with Adolf Hitler during
September 1938. But such narrow focus may fail to reveal broader
patterns in which those particular events occurred.

Schmitz examined appeasement and Munich as part of a much broader study of United States relations with Fascist Italy through nearly two decades from 1922 to 1940.[10] That broader study, along with his particular attention to the Italo-Ethiopian war and its aftermath, helped him escape from the narrow focus on Britain and Germany, and on Munich.

Schmitz provided an additional dimension and stretched the reader's thinking. Though Benito Mussolini's Fascist Italy provided one base for the Rome–Berlin Axis, Mussolini's Italy eventually joined Hitler's war against the West, and Mussolini and Italy suffered military defeat at the hands of Britain and the United States just as Germany and Japan did, those patterns may not necessarily have been inevitable. There were those in Europe, England, and the United States who remembered that Italy had fought on the Allied side in World War I, who believed Mussolini's fascism did not necessarily bind Italy to Hitler's Nazi Germany, and who recognized that even Italy could feel uneasy about its national security when the *Anschluss* early in 1938 expanded Nazi Germany's power to Italy's very borders. They hoped that a coalition of Great Britain, France, Italy, and possibly the Soviet Union (either within or outside of the League of Nations) might block potential German aggression and preserve a balance of power, security, and peace on the continent of Europe. In their separate ways in 1935 both the Stresa conference and the abortive Hoare-Laval accord pointed in those directions. President Roosevelt's ambassadors to Italy before World War II (Breckinridge Long from 1933 to 1936 and William Phillips from 1937 to 1941) both entertained hopes for some such arrangements in Europe.

Mussolini's aggressive warfare in East Africa in 1935–36, the League of Nations actions against Italy, and the growing accord between Hitler and Mussolini eroded that possibility in the eyes of many. Western opposition to Mussolini's ambitions in Africa drove the two dictators closer together and reduced the possibility of adding Italy to any coalition of states opposing Hitler's expanding ambitions in Europe and the world.

Nonetheless, Schmitz pointed to patterns of good relations

between the United States and Italy during the first dozen years that Mussolini and his Fascists ruled Italy. And he found evidence that more of that friendly relationship survived the Italo-Ethiopian war than most observers then and most historians since believed. He had no difficulty finding evidence to sustain his thesis in the views of Long, Phillips, and Welles. And those three (two of whom were career foreign service officers, members of the social elite in which FDR moved, and old friends of Roosevelt) were not without their influence on the president. President Roosevelt's last-minute appeal before the Munich conference to persuade Hitler to continue negotiations on the Sudetenland was channeled through Mussolini. The continuation of the Anglo-French nonintervention policies toward the Spanish Civil War even after Italian and German aid to Generalissimo Francisco Franco's forces was conspicuously apparent conceivably could be portrayed as appeasement of Mussolini's Fascist Italy (and Hitler's Nazi Germany). And though Schmitz did not carry his essay chronologically that far, Sumner Welles's diplomatic mission early in 1940 to explore possibilities for peace began and ended in Mussolini's Italy. Schmitz's analysis helps provide broader dimensions for understanding the entire story of the United States and appeasement in Europe in the 1930s.

Nonetheless, his analysis illustrates the difficulties inherent in the use of collective nouns and the definition of terms. Schmitz surely was correct about the views and hopes of Long, Phillips, Welles, and others. He was, however, less correct about Franklin D. Roosevelt at the top. Roosevelt did sign the Neutrality Act of 1935 into law and he did invoke that law with its mandatory arms embargo in the undeclared Italo-Ethiopian war. From the president's perspective, however, that was not appeasement. Without that neutrality legislation Italy would have had access to munitions and war goods produced in the United States. In contrast, primitive Abyssinia in east Africa lacked the wherewithal to buy or import from America. Consequently, the Neutrality Act of 1935 had the practical effect of depriving Italy of munitions it might have bought, while it deprived Ethiopia of nothing it could have obtained without the law. The list of munitions and war goods embargoed by the United States under Roosevelt was almost identical to the list of products denied Italy by League of Nations sanctions. Similarly, the practical effect of the administration's "moral embargo" was harmful to Italy and had no negative effects on Ethiopia.[11]

American isolationists thought the president was observing the noninterventionist spirit of the neutrality legislation when he invoked it in the Italo-Ethiopian war; Roosevelt, League leaders, and Mussolini knew better than that. Appearances clashed with reality. The reality was that under President Roosevelt the United States deliberately followed policies toward the Italo-Ethiopian war that preceded, paralleled, and reinforced the collective security sanctions imposed on Italy by the League of Nations led by Great Britain and France. That pattern further underscores Harrison's emphasis on FDR's efforts to lead the United States into diplomatic accord with Great Britain. Inadequate though the American embargo and League sanctions were to check Italian aggression in Africa, they did not constitute appeasement.[12]

Roosevelt had never really believed that enduring accord with Nazi Germany was possible. And he never really thought accord with Fascist Italy was terribly important one way or the other. It was Germany that Roosevelt saw as the terrible threat to European and world peace and security, not Italy. He was never much impressed by Italian power in Europe and the world—with or without Mussolini and his fascism. Roosevelt never gave the attention, priority, and effort to appeasing Mussolini and Italy that Ambassador Long, Ambassador Phillips, and Under Secretary Welles preferred. But then, Roosevelt never gave priority to American appeasement in Europe anyway, either as it was directed toward Germany or toward Italy. Ambassadors Long and Phillips may have fit Schmitz's thesis; President Franklin D. Roosevelt did not.

Schmitz's analysis also forces one to look squarely at what appeasement did and did not mean in the 1930s. If President Roosevelt had responded more favorably to the urgings of Long,

Phillips, and Welles to make positive efforts to win Mussolini's cooperation to encircle and check Nazi Germany and thereby preserve peace, that conceivably could be seen as power politics, realpolitik, or statecraft (depending on the circumstances)—but not necessarily appeasement. In any event, Long and Phillips did not succeed in their efforts to persuade the president. Welles's proposals for a conference did not materialize.[13]

Moreover, in authorizing the Welles mission to Europe early in 1940 the president had no serious expectation that it would result in a negotiated peace. President Roosevelt's goal in sending Welles almost certainly was to prove to the American people (including the isolationists and future historians) that he had made every possible effort for peace—that he had left nothing undone in his efforts to end the war. Welles's mission was part of FDR's continuing efforts to educate the American people away from their traditional isolationism toward a more active and positive role in world affairs. It had nothing to do with appeasement—of Mussolini, of Hitler, or even of American isolationists.[14]

Douglas Little's well-researched chapter of "Antibolshevism and Appeasement: Great Britain, the United States, and the Spanish Civil War," treats an additional dimension of the subject. Little focused on what he sees as "the intimate relationship during the late 1930s between antibolshevism and appeasement."

Adolf Hitler and his Nazis, Benito Mussolini and his Fascists, and Generalissimo Francisco Franco and his Nationalists all endangered democracy, freedom, peace, and security in Europe. From the perspective of many in the West, however, there was one thing good to be said about them—they all opposed communism and Stalin's Communist Russia. Analysts then and scholars since have pointed to the anti-Communist and anti-Soviet dimension of Chamberlain's appeasement policies. Fear of and hostility toward communism and the Soviet Union were significant elements in accounting for American foreign policies. Little properly inserts that part of the story into our thinking on the subject of appeasement.

Similarly, communism and Stalin challenged democracy, free enterprise, and freedom in the West. But there was one thing good to be said about them during much of the 1930. They opposed Nazi Germany, Fascist Italy, and Franco's Spanish Nationalists.

Many believed that Hitler's expansionist ambitions lay to the east in Europe rather than west toward France and Britain. And if that movement east led to war between Hitler's totalitarian Nazi Germany and Stalin's totalitarian Communist Soviet Union, few in the West would shed any tears. Similarly, Stalin and the Soviet Union would shed no tears if the Axis dictatorships and the Western democracies destroyed each other in warring against each other (as they were in the process of doing in 1939–41 before the Russo-German war began on June 22, 1941).

Much of that came together in the highly emotional debates in both Europe and the United States over policies toward the Spanish Civil War from 1936 to 1939. Erupting soon after the League of Nations had demonstrated its ineffectiveness in coping with the Italo-Ethiopian war, the Spanish Civil War conceivably could have engulfed Europe in the general war so many feared. With faith in the collective security formula of the League of Nations largely shattered, France and Great Britain tried to prevent the flames of the Spanish Civil War from spreading into a general war by organizing a twenty-seven-state Non-Intervention Committee— including Germany and Italy.

Tacitly and consciously paralleling and supplementing that effort, early in 1937 the Roosevelt administration pushed through Congress by near unanimous votes special legislation embargoing the sale of arms and munitions from the United States to both sides in the Spanish Civil War. The practical effect of both the Non-Intervention Committee in Europe and the Spanish embargo in the United States was to deprive the legally elected Loyalist republican government of Spain of outside sources of arms and munitions.

Three major European states, however, violated those efforts to isolate the fighting in Spain. The Soviet Union supplied aid to the Loyalist government of Spain, and Italy and Germany supplied material, planes, and men for Franco's Nationalist forces fighting against the Spanish government. The results worked at cross-purposes with British, French, and American policies and intentions. The consequences inflamed the Spanish Civil War into one of the bloodiest and most viciously contested civil clashes in modern European history, and made that civil war one of the most emotional international issues of modern times.

Little contends that the root explanation for the Anglo-French noninterventionist efforts and for the Spanish embargo enacted and enforced by the United States lay in the fear of the spread of communism. He advanced his thesis clearly and unequivocally in the very first paragraph of his chapter:

the British and American arms embargoes stemmed less from fear of a general European war than from suspicion that a Loyalist victory would open the door to bolshevism from the Aegean to the Atlantic. Furthermore, . . . those embargoes were never rescinded in large measure because non-intervention fit so well into the broader strategy of appeasement favored by most Foreign Office and State Department bureaucrats down through early 1939. Despite growing doubts among such high-ranking policy makers as Anthony Eden and Franklin Roosevelt, neither London nor Washington reversed course in Spain because too many other officials viewed fascism (whether in its German, Italian, or Spanish variant) as a useful antidote against alleged bolshevik subversion.

Through careful research both in England and in the United States he produced evidence of officials whose views were consistent with his interpretation. Both Sir Orme Sargent and Sir Samuel Hoare nicely fit Little's interpretation.

Little's interpretation serves at least three useful functions. Most important, it underscores the anti-Communist dimension of appeasement. Second, by taking sharp issue with more widely accepted interpretations Little forces the serious readers to rethink the whole subject. And third, his analysis vividly demonstrates the difficulty of determining truth about the past, and the comparative ease with which conscientious scholars can find data to give credence to widely varied historical interpretations.

The anti-Communist and anti-Soviet dimension of European appeasement in the 1930s was very real and significant. Little accurately cites contemporary documents to sustain his hypothesis. But relative to the total story, that dimension of policy toward the Spanish Civil War was comparatively small and inconspicuous. One can study hundreds of documents at the highest levels in the United States without finding much in the way of clear and unequivocal expressions of the reasoning that Little seized upon. Through painstaking research he produced "the needle in the haystack." He highlighted a neglected part of the past. But he was closer to the truth when he quoted Roosevelt in 1937 finding the basis for the mounting trouble in Europe "not in communism or the fear of communism but in Germany and the fear of what the present German leaders are . . . being drawn toward."

In my judgment, Little misinterprets the historical past by seizing on scattered bits of evidence that fit his hypothesis, by ignoring, minimizing, or discarding the more massive and substantial evidence that conflicts with his interpretation, and by attaching exaggerated weight to one small part of the data.

The old may not necessarily be right, and the new may not necessarily be wrong. But conversely, older interpretations may not necessarily be mistaken, and newer revisionist interpretations may not necessarily move one closer to the truth. Both government and private documents in both the United States and Great Britain fairly scream the contention that Britain and France, discouraged by the failure of the League's collective security sanctions in the Italo-Ethiopian war of 1935–36, and terrified at the possibility of a general war in Europe, desperately tried to insulate the Spanish Civil War to prevent it from spreading. And they persisted in those policies long after it was apparent that Italy, Germany, and the Soviet Union were blatantly violating those noninterventionist efforts, and long after it was apparent that their efforts were contributing to the triumph of Franco's Nationalists over the elected Loyalist republican government in Spain.

The Spanish embargo adopted by Congress at the urging of President Roosevelt, the Department of State, and the chairman of the Senate Foreign Relations Committee was a calculated effort to have the United States parallel and reinforce the Anglo-French efforts. In that sense the Spanish embargo meshes perfectly with the interpretation advanced by Harrison in his chapter of this book. When it became increasingly obvious both in Europe and in the United States that Italy, Germany, and the Soviet Union were shamelessly violating those noninterventionist efforts, opposition to the noninterventionist policies in Europe and to the Spanish embargo in America grew more vocal. Though many variables entered into the picture, so far as President Roosevelt was concerned he persisted with the Spanish embargo largely because of domestic politics. Repeal of the embargo in 1938 or early 1939 would have alienated the large Catholic population in the United States that passionately opposed the Loyalist government of Spain because of its anticlerical and anti-Church policies and actions. Not until Franco had triumphed decisively over the Loyalist republican government in Spain did the United States end its embargo on shipment of arms to Spain. But that embargo and its persistence were not for the most part inspired by appeasement considerations in America or by the determination to check the spread of communism in southern Europe "from the Aegean to the Atlantic."[15]

In conclusion, appeasement in the 1930s was largely a European policy, not an American policy. Though appeasement in Europe and isolationism in America had effects that inadvertently reinforced each other, they were not the same. There were those in the United States (and in the United States government) who sympathized with and applauded Neville Chamberlain's appeasement policies. Joseph P. Kennedy, United States ambassador to Great Britain from 1938 through 1940, was a conspicuous example. Most Americans (and most Europeans) felt a sense of relief when the Munich agreement temporarily averted a general war in Europe. The caution and inhibitions in foreign affairs that American isolationist strength forced on President Roosevelt helped move Chamberlain and other British and French leaders in their appeasement efforts.

Nonetheless, under Roosevelt's leadership the thrust of American policies toward Europe in the 1930s was not normally on behalf of appeasement. Even in the crucial days and hours preceding the Munich conference, President Roosevelt was careful not to endorse appeasement in general or any particular concessions or negotiating terms in particular. He urged only that negotiations be continued in the interests of peace. Roosevelt, like millions of others in Europe and the United States, felt a temporary sense of relief when the Munich Pact averted war at that time. But neither then nor earlier or later did Roosevelt really believe that appeasement could or would provide the formula for enduring peace in Europe and the world.

In 1938, Roosevelt knew that domestic politics and isolationist strength in the United States would not allow him to throw American might into a stronger, more positive role to block German aggression and to preserve peace in Europe and the world. To urge Britain and France to war to block German aggression in Czechoslovakia when he knew that he could not lead the United States to war on their side could be irresponsible and even immoral. The United States ambassador to France, William C. Bullitt, phrased that dilemma clearly in a message to Secretary of State Cordell Hull in the midst of the crises leading up to the Munich conference: "It is entirely honorable to urge another nation to go to war if one is prepared to war at once on the side of that nation but I know of nothing more dishonorable than to urge another nation to go to war if one is determined not to go to war on the side of that nation, and I believe that the people of the United States are determined not to go to war against Germany."[16] Roosevelt, Hull, Chamberlain, Daladier, and Hitler all knew that Bullitt was correct at that time on that issue. That reality made appeasement in Europe seem more essential in the eyes of Chamberlain and Daladier than it would have seemed otherwise. And that situation made it impossible for Roosevelt to pursue policies in Europe that might have had better long-term consequences than appeasement.

In summary, Roosevelt was not an appeaser. Under the circumstances he could hope that Chamberlain's appeasement policies might produce enduring peace in Europe and the world. But he did not really believe that they would. And at that time there was nothing he could do to put into operation the policies he might have preferred.

NOTES

1. Surprisingly, many of the relevant memoirs from that era, biographies of Chamberlain and others involved, and scholarly histories of Munich and appeasement neglect to provide precise definitions of the term—or even include it in the index. Among the better scholarly historical definitions of appeasement is in William R. Rock, *Appeasement on Trial: British Foreign Policy and Its Critics, 1938–1939* (Hamden, Conn.: Archon Books, 1966), pp. 3–4, 8–9, 11, 337–38. For an excellent contemporary definition by one who participated in and approved of the policy, see Lothian (Philip Henry Kerr) to Felix Frankfurter, May 10, 1939, Felix Frankfurter Papers, Library of Congress, Washington, D.C.
2. Keith Feiling, *The Life of Neville Chamberlain* (London: Macmillan, 1970), p. 326.
3. On this subject, see Wayne S. Cole, *Roosevelt and the Isolationists, 1932–45* (Lincoln: University of Nebraska Press, 1983).
4. Feiling, *Chamberlain*, p. 325. See also Cole, *Roosevelt and the Isolationists*, pp. 249, 301.
5. Cole, *Roosevelt and the Isolationists*, pp. 396–401.
6. For my own general perspective on the subject, written more than twenty years ago, see Wayne S. Cole, *An Interpretive History of American Foreign Relations* (Homewood, Ill.: Dorsey Press, 1968), pp. 438–41.
7. Elliott Roosevelt, ed., *F.D.R.: His Personal Letters, 1928–1945*, 2 vols. (New York: Duell, Sloan and Pearce, 1950), vol. 1, p. 571.
8. Cole, *Roosevelt and the Isolationists*, pp. 4–6, 246–49, 297–309.
9. For my own treatment of Joseph P. Kennedy and his roles as both an appeaser and an isolationist, see Cole, *Roosevelt and the Isolationists*, pp. 275–90.
10. David F. Schmitz, *The United States and Fascist Italy, 1922–1940* (Chapel Hill: University of North Carolina Press, 1988).
11. A. J. Drexel Biddle, Jr. to Secretary of State, October 21, 1935, File Number 757.65/2, Record Group 59, Department of State Records, National Archives, Washington, D.C.; Robert A. Divine, *The Illusion of Neutrality* (Chicago: University of Chicago Press, 1962), pp. 122–34; Cole, *Roosevelt and the Isolationists*, pp. 180–82.
12. Divine, *Illusion of Neutrality*, pp. 122–34; Cole, *Roosevelt and the Isolationists*, pp. 180–82.

13. In addition to the scholarly accounts cited in Schmitz's chapter, on this subject my thinking has benefited from two excellent theses, both based on impressive research in archival and manuscript materials: Caroline Keith Ehlers, "William Phillips: The Failure of a Mission" (M.A. thesis, University of Maryland, 1979); and Mary Jo Tudor, "President Roosevelt's Peace Moves in Europe, September 1937 to May 1939" (M.A. thesis, University of Maryland, 1967).

14. Cole, *Roosevelt and the Isolationists*, pp. 338–42.

15. For a fuller account of my data and perspectives on United States policies toward the Spanish Civil War, see Cole, *Roosevelt and the Isolationists*, pp. 223–30, 234–38. See also *Foreign Relations of the United States: Diplomatic Papers, 1937*, 5 vols. (Washington, D.C.: Government Printing Office, 1954), vol. 1, pp. 353–55, 374–76.

16. *Foreign Relations of the United States: Diplomatic Papers, 1938*, 5 vols. (Washington, D.C.: Government Printing Office, 1955), vol. 1, p. 618.

2

Antibolshevism and Appeasement: Great Britain, the United States, and the Spanish Civil War

Douglas Little

Half a century ago, Spain was rocked by a bloody upheaval which many have come to regard as the opening round of World War II. Both the United States and Great Britain adopted policies of strict nonintervention in August 1936, not only denying the Spanish Republic the weapons it needed so desperately to put down General Franco's rebellion, but also setting the stage for subsequent efforts to appease his chief supporters, Hitler and Mussolini. I wish to suggest here that the British and American arms embargoes stemmed less from fear of a general European war than from suspicion that a Loyalist victory would open the door to bolshevism from the Aegean to the Atlantic. Furthermore, I would argue that those embargoes were never rescinded, in large measure because nonintervention fit so well into the broader strategy of appeasement favored by most Foreign Office and State Department bureaucrats down through early 1939. Despite growing doubts among such high-ranking policymakers as Anthony Eden and Franklin Roosevelt, neither London nor Washington reversed course in Spain because too many other officials viewed fascism (whether in its German, Italian, or Spanish variant) as a useful antidote against alleged Bolshevik subversion.[1]

From its very inception in 1931, the Spanish Republic found little favor in Washington or London. The deepening global depression had hit Spain especially hard, prompting the new regime to flirt with autarchic policies detrimental to important British and American interests. The State Department and the Foreign Office were extremely sensitive about the fate of the quarter billion dollars invested in Spain by U.S. and U.K. firms, and each intervened repeatedly at Madrid on behalf of such multinational giants as International Telephone and Telegraph and Rio Tinto, both of which were targeted for expropriation in the early 1930s. Spain's efforts to curb its huge trade deficit by imposing discriminatory import quotas, surcharges, and exchange controls, first against the United States and later against Great Britain, added insult to injury. As a result, by the spring of 1936 British and American economic relations with Spain bordered on commercial cold war.[2]

Such threats to American and British economic interests, however, paled before more pressing ideological concerns. Put most simply, there was on the eve of the Spanish Civil War widespread suspicion in both London and Washington that the republic was little more than a stalking horse for communism throughout the Mediterranean. As early as 1931, American diplomats had reported "widespread Bolshevistic influences" at Madrid, while their British counterparts worried that "Spain would go down a slippery slope into bolshevism." Although the Spanish Communist Party then claimed fewer than a thousand members, such prophecies did not seem far-fetched in light of the political turmoil which plagued Spain over the ensuing five years. Nor was the narrow victory of the Communist-backed Popular Front coalition in the Spanish elections of February 1936 likely to inspire much confidence.[3]

Indeed, both the Foreign Office and the State Department drew sinister parallels between the Spanish Popular Front and the anti-fascist "united front" strategy adopted by the Comintern in Moscow the preceding August. Moreover, the rapid growth of Spain's Communist party, whose membership was rumored in early 1936 to exceed thirty thousand, rekindled all their earlier suspicions about Bolshevik subversion. With the approach of spring, ITT prepared for renewed left-wing assaults, U.S. military intelligence detected signs of increased Comintern activity, and Ambassador

Claude Bowers, a Jeffersonian liberal sympathetic to the Spanish left, worried privately that "there are communistic elements in Spain that are working toward another French Revolution with its Terror."[4] Rio Tinto and other British firms likewise braced themselves for a new wave of violence, the British embassy compared conditions in Spain to "those in Russia prior to the Bolshevik Revolution," and Ambassador Henry Chilton warned that there were plans afoot to "set up a Soviet Republic."[5]

This deepening turmoil in Spain gradually forced British and American policymakers to contemplate the even more frightful possibility that Soviet subversion might spread throughout Southern Europe. U.S. diplomats, for example, were already extremely sensitive about possible Communist inroads in Italy. Ambassador Breckinridge Long feared in late 1935 that Mussolini's high-risk policy in Ethiopia might backfire and spark "manifestations of Bolshevism" in Rome. Early in 1936 Pierrepont Moffat, the once and future chief of the State Department's Western European division, worried that an Italian defeat would bring "revolution in Italy, with communism or near communism thrust into the heart of Europe."[6] British officials were equally concerned about the situation in Lisbon, where the Salazar regime was charging that "Spain was moving fast towards Communism" which "would be exceedingly serious for Portugal." Foreign Secretary Eden was alarmed by the growth of a "Communist movement in Portugal," and subsequent reports from British diplomats in the Iberian Peninsula during the spring of 1936 confirmed that Lisbon was "the natural prey of any Communist government" at Madrid.[7] The situation in Athens, where the Greek Popular Front launched a violent campaign in April against King George and his royalist regime, was of equal concern. Ambassador Lincoln MacVeagh advised the White House that "Communistic agitators" and "broadcasts from Moscow" were responsible for the attack, an interpretation shared by his British colleague, Sir Sydney Waterlow, who quietly encouraged General Ioannis Metaxas to seize power the following August.[8]

Conditions in France, where socialist leader Leon Blum and his

Popular Front coalition had swept to victory on May 3, 1936, looked even grimmer. As early as March 20 Breckinridge Long in Rome had warned Under Secretary of State and soon-to-be Ambassador to Italy William Phillips that the Soviet Union had recently established "an important internal political nucleus in France" and would soon be "exerting her influence through her political organization in Paris to serve the purpose of Moscow." Jesse Straus, ambassador to France, tried to be more optimistic, assuring Roosevelt and Secretary of State Cordell Hull in May that Blum's regime would probably resemble "something akin to your New Deal" and that no communists would join the cabinet. The president, however, was deeply disturbed by the wave of sit-down strikes which rocked France in early June and instructed Straus to delay his return to Washington until this "very serious trouble" had subsided.[9]

The British government at Whitehall was even less sanguine than the White House. When Permanent Under Secretary of State Robert Vansittart cabled Paris on June 10 to ask "how far the swing to the Left has really gone," Ambassador George Clerk did not mince words. "It is extraordinarily reminiscent of the early days of the Russian Revolution," he replied the next day, "with Blum as an unconscious Kerensky and an unknown Lenin or Trotsky in the background." Clerk's views merely confirmed what Foreign Office experts such as Orme Sargent had suspected all along: the Soviets were "still pursuing the old Bolshevist policy, *which is to sow trouble in Europe generally in the hope of being able to reap a harvest of communism.*" After underscoring Sargent's remarks, Eden scrawled "I agree" and had Clerk's dispatch printed for circulation to the cabinet.[10]

If British and American policymakers regarded conditions from Lisbon to Paris as ominous, by the summer of 1936 they regarded the situation at Madrid as nothing short of appalling. Ruthless bands of left- and right-wing gunmen battled in the streets; sit-down strikes and sabotage plagued ITT, Rio Tinto, and other foreign firms; and rumors of Comintern subversion circulated among the diplomatic corps. U.S. Ambassador William Bullitt, on

leave pending reassignment from Moscow to Paris, lent credence
to such rumors. In London he told influential Tories that "Moscow
foretells a Communist government in Spain in three months." Later
in Washington he advised Phillips that "Russia is still actively
pursuing her international policy of Sovietizing other countries and
has recently sent out a large number of Soviet agents supplied with
ample funds to Spain."[11]
These accounts and others like them left few doubts on either
side of the Atlantic that the Spanish Republic was teetering on the
brink of a proletarian revolution. James Dunn, Hull's confidant
and top adviser on European affairs, complained in June that the
Popular Front in Madrid was doing little to combat the Communists and that, as a result, "the masses are getting out of hand."
Likewise convinced that Spain's left-wing government was "either
afraid or powerless to maintain order" in the face of "Communist"
disturbances, Whitehall's Robert Vansittart termed conditions at
Madrid "disgraceful" and warned Eden on June 24 that events
were "taking a turn detrimental to British interests."[12]
Just how detrimental became obvious a month later, when
General Franco launched a military uprising which plunged Spain
into a civil war that many had come to regard as inevitable. The
Spanish Popular Front turned at once to its French counterpart for
support, and Premier Blum agreed without hesitation to supply the
weapons necessary to combat Franco's rebels. When Blum arrived
in London shortly afterward for a long-scheduled meeting with
British officials, however, he met "strong pro-Rebel feeling in the
British cabinet" and was urged by Eden and others to be extremely
cautious. Privately, Prime Minister Stanley Baldwin was much
blunter about Blum's "meddling" in Spain. "I told Eden yester-
day," Baldwin remarked over lunch on July 27, "that on no account, French or other, must he bring us into the fight on the side
of the Russians." Well aware of such British displeasure, Blum
returned to Paris, consulted his own cabinet, and reluctantly halted
French arms sales to Spain later that same day.[13]
Its lifeline to France severed, Madrid turned next to Washington.
Alarmed by the Popular Front's decision to distribute "large quan-

tities of arms and ammunition into the hands of irresponsible members of Left-Wing political organizations," Hull warned Roosevelt in late July that should the military uprising fail, "mob rule and anarchy would follow." Despite mounting evidence of German and Italian aid to Franco, neither Hull nor Phillips was eager to assist the increasingly isolated Loyalists. "If they cannot get such supplies in Europe, they will undoubtedly turn to us and we shall be in an embarrassing situation since we have no legislation authorizing us to refuse the export of such materials even though they are destined for what amounts to a communistic government," Phillips remarked privately after several long conferences with Hull on August 4. "The critical part of the situation is that if the [Spanish] Government wins, as now seems likely, communism throughout Europe will be immensely stimulated." Consequently, the State Department imposed an informal "moral embargo" on all arms shipments to Spain the next day, and when pressed for a formal ruling, Hull and Phillips persuaded Roosevelt to make nonintervention public on August 11.[14]

Four days later, for remarkably similar reasons, Britain likewise adopted a policy of strict nonintervention. Increasingly convinced that a Loyalist victory would plunge Spain into "the chaos of some form of bolshevism," British officials were worried in early August that France was drifting away from its policy of "official neutrality." Blum was under intense left-wing pressure to assist the Loyalists, raising the specter of what Orme Sargent called "a France weakened or paralyzed by Communistic infection" and strengthening the conviction that Britain must prevent the French "by hook or by crook from 'going bolshevik' under the influence of the Spanish Civil War." The simplest way to help France "free itself from communist domination, both domestic and Muscovite" was to create a multilateral system of nonintervention which would, as Whitehall's number three man Alexander Cadogan put it, "prevent Bolshevism in Spain" and also avoid Blum's "own overthrow by Bolshevism in France."[15]

On August 14 Eden phoned Lord Halifax from Yorkshire for an update on the Spanish crisis. Halifax, who as minister without

portfolio oversaw the Foreign Office in Eden's absence, stressed
that nonintervention might bridge the fundamental differences
between the great powers by "our all making agreement on a
non-Communist Govt" at Madrid. "For we certainly—nor we
presume the French—do *not* want to see a Communist Govt
established in Spain," he pointed out. "And *that* we appreciate—
and we understand their position—is the principal anxiety of Italy
& Germany." With Blum still wavering on French neutrality, Eden
agreed that nonintervention must be implemented at once, and the
following morning Britain and France exchanged notes pledging
"rigorously [to] abstain from all interference, direct or indirect, in
the internal affairs of Spain."[16]

Italy and Germany soon made similar pledges and agreed to
participate in the newly created Non-Intervention Committee that
met regularly in London. But Eden remained fearful that "this
Spanish horror" would polarize European politics still further.
Appalled by the prospect of "France growing more 'Red'," he
noted that Britons could no longer "take comfort that this process
cannot be rapid," because "it is precisely in this respect that the
Spanish peril plays its part." For Eden, Spain had become an
ideological Pandora's box. "If events in that country & the failure
of non-intervention force the less extreme elements in the French
government to resign," he asked himself, "what must the conse-
quence be?"[17]

The answer to Eden's rhetorical question reverberated through
the diplomatic chanceries on both sides of the Atlantic. At the
Foreign Office, there was with the approach of winter little doubt
that, in the words of one official, "the alternative to Franco is
communism tempered with anarchy, and if this last regime is
triumphant in Spain it will spread to other countries, notably
France." Indeed, as late as New Year's Eve Vansittart charged that
the Kremlin was working hard in Spain to ensure "the victory of
the Left—a very extreme Left—which would spread a dividing
and disintegrating contagion into France and from France to
ourselves."[18]

Ironically, however, the nonintervention policies pursued by

Britain and the United States actually did more to accelerate than to contain the Communist "contagion," not only in Spain but elsewhere as well. As Italian troops and German equipment carried Franco's insurgents to the gates of Madrid in late 1936, only the Soviet Union came to the aid of the Spanish Loyalists. Russian tanks and planes began to arrive in October, soon to be followed by the first contingents of the International Brigades, an army of fifty thousand left-wing volunteers recruited by the Comintern from over thirty countries. As the Kremlin's critical role in defending Spanish democracy became clear, Communist prestige soared among anti-Fascist liberals and radicals from Paris to Mexico City while the republican regime in Madrid drifted steadily leftward.[19]

Belittling the self-fulfilling aspects of their own policy of nonintervention, top U.S. officials soon detected signs of clandestine Soviet efforts to circumvent the informal American ban on arms sales to Loyalist Spain. In early December, rumors began to circulate that Robert Cuse, a Russian-born Jersey City arms broker who headed the Vimalert Company, intended to ignore the "moral embargo" and ship badly needed aircraft to the Spanish Republic. Even worse, Robert Kelley, chief of the State Department's Division of Eastern European Affairs, learned from Federal Bureau of Investigation Director J. Edgar Hoover that Vimalert personnel had close ties with Amtorg, the Soviet trading agency in the United States.[20] Lacking legal grounds to block Cuse's proposed sale, the State Department issued the necessary export licenses on December 29. The next day, however, Acting Secretary of State R. Walton Moore visited the White House with Hull's blessing and persuaded Roosevelt to seek tough new legislation barring all arms sales to both sides in the Spanish conflict. With the passage of the Spanish Embargo Act of January 8, 1937, aiding republican Spain became not just highly irregular but also strictly illegal.[21]

Because it was obvious that Hitler and Mussolini had no intention of honoring their earlier pledges to halt their assistance to Franco, friends of the Spanish Republic showered criticism on the American embargo. Roosevelt was bombarded by angry telegrams and letters, some from Socialist luminaries like Norman Thomas and Albert Einstein urging him to scuttle nonintervention, others from angry men in the street like George Greig of Yakima, Washington, who accused pro-Fascists in the State Department of "slipping over the embargo on armaments to the democratically elected government of Spain."[22] Such barbs, however, merely led Hull and his subordinates to redouble their efforts to ensure America's continued noninvolvement in the Spanish Civil War. After all, State Department munitions controller Joseph Green recalled seven years later, only "a very small group, mostly Communists and Extreme Left Wingers," had opposed the embargo.[23]

These left-wing jeremiads directed against the State Department bureaucracy worked further to discredit the Loyalist cause among top U.S. policymakers. Most American diplomats, with the notable exception of the liberal Bowers, believed the Spanish Republic was trapped, as one put it, "in the coils of the communistic serpent." Sumner Welles, who became under secretary after Phillips departed for his new post in Italy in the autumn of 1936, admitted candidly long afterward that Loyalist links to the Communists had "created suspicion and hostility" at the State Department. "From the outset of hostilities," one middle-level bureaucrat confirmed much later, "high echelon officials were strongly pro-Franco."[24] So were corporations like ITT, whose executives were "very partisan to the rebels" and pressed the State Department to keep its distance from "the Spanish radicals and the Soviet crowd" in republican Madrid.[25]

By early 1937, however, Roosevelt was less concerned about Soviet inroads among the Loyalists than about the increasingly brazen German and Italian military aid for Franco. "The President talked a bit about Europe," *The New York Times* correspondent Arthur Krock noted after a private White House visit. "He is concerned over the number of Italians in Spain—20,000 fighting men at least, he had heard."[26] Phillips, an old friend and Harvard classmate, assured Roosevelt from Rome that nonintervention remained the wisest course and emphasized that Mussolini had become involved only because he claimed to have "proof positive of communist ambitions in the Mediterranean which are intended to spread to France." But the president's doubts persisted. The basis for the mounting trouble in Europe, he told Phillips on February 6, "lies, *I* think, not in communism or the fear of communism but in Germany and the fear of what the present German leaders are . . . being drawn toward."[27]

Some cabinet members shared Roosevelt's growing sense of uneasiness about U.S. policy toward Spain. Interior Secretary Harold Ickes, for example, complained as early as March 15 that Hull's recent decision to broaden the embargo to prevent American medical assistance from reaching the Loyalists was "really an unneutral act" that "makes me ashamed."[28] Treasury Secretary Henry Morgenthau was likewise deeply troubled by a policy which seemed increasingly to play into the hands of Nazi Germany.[29] The State Department, however, remained more committed than ever to nonintervention, and worked closely behind the scenes with like-minded leaders on Capitol Hill to incorporate key aspects of the Spanish embargo into the general Neutrality Act that Congress passed on May 1, 1937.[30] As before, Hull and his top aides were motivated as much by their dislike of the left-wing Loyalist regime as by any fear of a wider war. "We here look upon the Spanish Government as a lot of hoodlums," James Dunn, who now headed the Department's Division of Western European Affairs, told a reporter in March 1937 while "Hull nodded his head in approval."[31] Nor did Hull disagree when Portuguese Ambassador Jose Antonio de Bianchi charged several months later that republican Spain "is controlled by the Reds or Communists" and that "the Soviet is more or less directing the situation."[32]

Claude Bowers could not have disagreed more. From his "embassy-in-exile" across the French border at St. Jean de Luz, he had been warning the White House for nearly a year that the Spanish Civil War was a fight to the death between fascism and democracy, not between nationalism and communism. Portugal's Antonio Salazar, like Hitler and Mussolini, was making a mockery of nonintervention. "We know damn well that Italy and Germany are at war with Spain—but we sell them arms and ammunition," Bowers exploded privately on June 24. "And we, too, set aside international law by refusing to sell [arms] to the legal constitutional Government of Spain."[33] A few days later Norman Thomas urged the president to use the discretionary powers spelled out in the new Neutrality Act to embargo all U.S. war materiel bound for Italy and Germany. Impressed by such similar criticism from two such different sources, Roosevelt told Hull on June 29 that if Hitler and Mussolini were "actually taking part in the fighting in Spain on the side of Franco, . . . then in such case we shall have to act under the Neutrality Act."[34]

Unable to deny wholesale German and Italian violations of the nonintervention agreement, the State Department argued instead that the president's proposal would drive Berlin and Rome closer together at precisely the moment that both Britain and the United States were working to keep them apart. "Italy is in a favorable position to put the brakes on Germany should a crisis arise," Phillips had reminded Roosevelt in an April apologia for Mussolini's actions in Spain.[35] Ambassador Robert Bingham in London confirmed in early July that Whitehall still hoped to woo Mussolini away from Hitler by keeping the Spanish conflict "localized" and added that Britain opposed any American sanctions for the time being. Once British opposition became clear, the president agreed to scrap his plan to broaden the Spanish embargo because, as Eden noted on July 6, "Roosevelt desired to do nothing without first consulting us."[36]

British policy toward Spain during the summer of 1937 was still guided by the same blend of anticommunism and bureaucratic inertia which shaped American nonintervention. To be sure, Eden had questioned the wisdom of this policy as early as January 8, when he suggested that the Cabinet approve a plan calling for greater British vigilance in enforcing the arms embargo against the Spanish rebels. But his subordinates at the Foreign Office believed such steps would only prolong the war and delay the restoration of law and order, as did Cabinet rivals such as first Lord of the Admiralty Samuel Hoare, who complained that Eden's proposal would create "a situation where, as a nation, we were trying to stop General Franco from winning." When Eden pointed out that continued German and Italian meddling in Spain seemed certain to generate "a great deal of complaint" among the Labour opposition, Minister of Health Sir Kingsley Wood retorted that "many people in this country would be equally troubled if the Bolshevists achieved a victory."[37]

British officials made no secret of their pro-Franco leanings in private talks with Americans both inside and outside government. Sir Gerald Campbell, Britain's Consul General in Washington, discussed the situation in Spain over lunch on January 4 with former Secretary of State Henry Stimson and "got into a discussion as to which was more dangerous—Communism or Fascism." The British "seemed to think that communism was more dangerous," Stimson noted in his diary that evening, and "were afraid that if Spain went communistic it would communize France."[38] A month later Mahlon Perkins, the American Consul in Barcelona, confirmed that local British representatives believed a Loyalist victory would produce "a Spain more or less 'Bolshevized,' which, apart from political considerations, would menace British investments in the country and the normal continuance of commercial intercourse."[39]

Claude Bowers likewise reported on February 23 that Sir Henry Chilton, his British counterpart, was quietly establishing informal ties with Franco's rebels with an eye to protecting Britain's commercial interests after the war.[40] Indeed, few British officials would have taken issue with First Sea Lord Sir Ernle Chatfield, who told a friend about this time that "I do not see how Franco can help winning, because one feels that he has a much nobler cause than the Reds."[41]

The British left, however, had serious questions about the nobility of Franco's cause. Although Clement Attlee, Hugh Dalton, and other Labour party leaders initially shared some of the Tory misgivings that Communist subversion in Spain would ignite a wider war, left-wing firebrands like Ellen Wilkinson and Aneuran Bevan hammered away at nonintervention during the autumn of 1936 as both grossly unfair to the Loyalists and manifestly unwise for British security interests. By February 1937, a crack battalion of nearly two thousand British International Brigaders, two-thirds of them Communists, was holding off an Italian force nearly twice as large at Jarama, while in London Socialist Leaguer Sir Stafford Cripps was launching a drive to rescind Britain's embargo on arms sales to republican Spain. And as Hitler and Mussolini's assistance for Franco began to tilt the balance inexorably toward a rebel victory in the spring of 1937, both the Labour Party and the Trade Unions Congress at last urged Neville Chamberlain, Baldwin's heir apparent as prime minister, to reconsider the policy of nonintervention.[42]

Influential Conservatives both inside and outside the cabinet, however, pressed the new prime minister to reaffirm his predecessor's policies in Spain. Sir Samuel Hoare, for example, acknowledged the "difficulty of maintaining non-intervention" in the face of mounting criticism from the "hysterical left," but urged Chamberlain as early as March 1937 to do nothing in Spain that might impede a broader "European reconciliation" with Germany and Italy.[43] Nor were Tory backbenchers bashful in voicing their hopes for a right-wing victory over the Spanish Loyalists. In mid-July Sir Harold Nicolson, a lonely Conservative critic of appeasement, remarked that the majority were "passionately anti-Government and pro-Franco." Not surprisingly, U.S. diplomats in London confirmed later that summer that although Chamberlain was well aware of German and Italian violations of nonintervention, he was beginning "to trim sails for the possibility of a Franco victory" and was already "preparing public opinion for an eventual recognition of Franco."[44]

By the autumn of 1937, however, both Foreign Secretary Eden and Permanent Under Secretary Vansittart had begun to have serious reservations about appeasing Hitler and Mussolini in Spain as an antidote to bolshevism. Disturbed by such increasingly blatant Italian intervention as the "piratical" attacks carried out against Loyalist shipping in the western Mediterranean by supposedly "unknown" submarines, Eden took the lead in negotiating the Nyon Agreement of September 14, 1937, which stepped up British and French naval patrols along those sections of the Spanish coast plagued by undersea raids.[45] Two weeks later Vansittart confessed that Mussolini's continued meddling in Spain was now "undoubtedly a danger to our interests" and argued that Whitehall must endorse the Quai d'Orsay's recent proposal to send a stiff new Anglo-French demarche to Italy.[46]

Eden agreed that "a joint note was necessary and inevitable," but others at the Foreign Office resisted such "questionable" action. Convinced that the proposed demarche would "lead to the denunciation by ourselves and France of the non-intervention policy," Sir Orme Sargent contended that only the Kremlin stood to benefit from an Anglo-Italian breach. "Again (though I hesitate to produce again my King Charles's head)," he wondered whether the French, "in proposing direct action against Italy, are the victims of pressure from the Russian Government, who can threaten not only to withdraw the Communist vote from the [Blum] Government, but also to dislocate the already precarious economic situation in France by a recrudescence of strikes, etc.?"[47]

Nor were high-ranking members of the British Government eager to embrace the pro-French and anti-Italian policy Eden unveiled at a cabinet meeting on October 13. French anxieties about Italy's intentions in the Western Mediterranean "were by no means unjustified," Eden pointed out, inasmuch as Mussolini had provided Franco with "large military formations and Italian Generals whose photographs could be seen in any cinema in Europe." This being so, it was necessary for Britain to work closely with France under the auspices of the Non-Intervention Committee to secure the withdrawal of the Italian expeditionary force, with the understanding that should the Duce prove uncooperative, "we should reserve our liberty of action."[48]

But Sir Samuel Hoare, now Chamberlain's home secretary, dissented, arguing that Eden's scheme virtually guaranteed the breakdown of nonintervention and "the formation of an Anglo-French-Russian bloc" inimical to Britain's interests. Colonial Minister William Ormsby-Gore agreed, adding that he "did not think that British public opinion was at all anxious" to see "Great Britain and Russia [get] together." And Oliver Stanley, president of the

Board of Trade, was "rather horrified" by Eden's statements "casting aspersions on Italian good faith" and complained that "we were drifting near to a position of having to say that General Franco must not be allowed to win." With no consensus in sight, Prime Minister Chamberlain suggested that the wisest course seemed for Britain to keep its distance from France, press for the withdrawal of all foreign troops (both pro-Loyalist and pro-Franco), and thereby avoid antagonizing Mussolini.[49] Both Eden and Vansittart continued to insist that a rebel victory would play into the hands of an increasingly formidable Berlin–Rome axis, but with the approach of winter the appeasers regained the upper hand inside Whitehall. Orme Sargent, for example, complained privately that "the S of S [secretary of state] and Van [Vansittart] have come round to the view that a Franco victory . . . would be contrary to our interests." Predictably, he also expressed relief that their plan to step up Anglo-French pressure on Mussolini to withdraw from Spain "has been meeting with considerable opposition" within the cabinet from Hoare and others who "object to having our Spanish policy dictated by France (and particularly a Socialist France)."[50] When Eden wondered whether the League of Nations might play a greater role in resolving conflicts like the one in Spain, Alexander Cadogan retorted that "in its present maimed state" the League actually did "more harm than good," because "it serves simply as a meeting ground for the 'Democracies,' at which Spaniards, Ethiopians, and Chinese state their grievances."[51] Once Vansittart's criticism of appeasement in Spain and elsewhere grew too strident, Prime Minister Chamberlain "promoted" him to the largely honorific post of chief diplomatic adviser in December 1937 and tapped the "sane, slow" Cadogan to replace him as permanent under secretary. Eden was now almost totally isolated, and after wrangling with Chamberlain over appeasement in general and Mussolini's Spanish adventure in particular, he resigned in February 1938 and was succeeded as foreign secretary by the more conservative Lord Halifax.[52]

Ever suspicious of the European left, both Cadogan and Halifax remained committed, as they had been since August 1936, to nonintervention in Spain and appeasement in Europe. Cadogan, for example, took the lead in scuttling a Kremlin proposal for an Anglo-Soviet pact against Nazi Germany in March 1938. "The Russian object is to precipitate confusion and war in Europe," he wrote tersely with his gaze fixed on Spain. "They will hope for the world revolution as a result (and a very likely one, too)." And when Vansittart charged four months later that those who still favored nonintervention were "living in a fool's paradise" oblivious to the mounting Fascist threat which had long since superseded any Communist menace, Halifax retorted that "we are, in the circumstances, pursuing the right policy" in Spain. "Personally," he added, "I am of the opinion that Franco is bound to win at some time or another. To encourage the sending of material to the [Loyalist] Government would not only be contrary to our policy of Non-Intervention, but would also inevitably prolong the war with additional dangerous possibilities."[53]

Similar bureaucratic and ideological obstacles on the other side of the Atlantic prevented President Roosevelt, who shared many of Eden's and Vansittart's growing doubts about appeasement in Spain, from lifting the American embargo on arms to the Spanish Loyalists. Down through the spring of 1938, U.S. policy remained firmly in the hands of such influential State Department anti-Communists as Pierrepont Moffat and James Dunn, who believed that a Loyalist victory would stimulate bolshevism throughout Europe. When Dunn returned to Washington in September 1937 from a whirlwind tour of the continent, for example, he dismissed the growing public outcry against Mussolini as shortsighted. "We considered that Italy had intervened in Spain in an offensive and aggressive manner," he explained privately to Moffat, "whereas they considered that Russia had intervened in Spain and that they were merely acting defensively."[54] The Bureau of Foreign and Domestic Commerce echoed State Department concerns about Soviet subversion and warned that a Loyalist victory would mean "capitalism will be banned (as it has already in Barcelona), and in this case the value of foreign investments and credits will be extremely doubtful."[55] Nor were American firms operating in

Spain optimistic about the consequences of a republican victory in
the civil war. "Should the Loyalists win," ITT executives told
Moffat in January 1938, "the more moderate elements" would be
unable to control "the Communists," and "the center of gravity
would be very much farther to the Left."[56]

Other Americans, however, were even more disturbed by the
likely consequences of a Franco victory. Troubled by rumors that
"there is a Fascist clique in the [State] Department," Claude
Bowers warned Roosevelt from his embassy-in-exile at St. Jean
de Luz in late February that it was becoming "difficult for us to
justify our refusal . . . to permit the constitutional Spanish Government to buy arms and ammunition" now that even the Non-Intervention Committee acknowledged that Germany and Italy were
using Spain as "a laboratory for the testing of the efficiency of their
improved methods of destruction." The president "hate[d] to think
of the war in Spain as a mere laboratory" and pressed the State
Department to send Bowers to Barcelona, a key Loyalist strong-
hold, to demonstrate American opposition to German and Italian
aggression.[57]

But Hull and his staff were extremely reluctant to take any steps
which might shore up a Loyalist regime they regarded as little more
than a stalking horse for Soviet subversion. Less concerned about
Hitler's and Mussolini's intervention in Spain than about the
increasingly brutal and unpredictable behavior of Joseph Stalin,
Chief of the Division of European Affairs Pierrepont Moffat was
convinced by early 1938 that "the Comintern is to be reorganized
on a much more efficient basis and the idea of world revolution is
to be pushed not on a grandiose scale but with renewed vigor and
intelligence at key points." Since Spain seemed likely to be one of
those points, he opposed Roosevelt's plan to station Bowers at
Barcelona. Well aware that such action "would be construed under
present conditions as a move to bolster up the Loyalist Government
despite our policy of nonintervention," the State Department managed to persuade the White House on March 14 to keep Bowers at
St. Jean de Luz until the military situation in Barcelona stabilized.

This "would give us two or three months," Moffat noted privately, "to see whether the Franco offensive would end matters."[58]

Before the spring was out, however, Roosevelt contemplated bolstering up the Loyalists in much more dramatic fashion by repealing the year-old embargo on arms sales to Spain. Long-time Socialist and liberal critics of nonintervention were now joined by a broader cross section of Americans, including many Catholics, who were appalled by the German terror bombing of Guernica and the ruthless Italian treatment of Loyalist prisoners of war. Journalists as diverse as Drew Pearson and Max Lerner attacked the State Department architects of nonintervention as "pro-Fascist career men who were strangling democracy in Spain."[59] More to the point, such New Deal insiders as Harold Ickes and Henry Morgenthau believed the president had the authority to repeal the arms embargo under the terms of the Neutrality Act of 1937 and urged him to do just that.[60]

But when Roosevelt consulted the State Department in late March, Hull and his top aides dug in their heels. "After thrashing the thing out pro and con," Moffat noted on March 31, "the Secretary felt that we should not take as firm a stand as sound policy dictated for the simple reason that he thought the president would overrule us on an emotional appeal from the entire Left-Wing in this country." Instead of arguing the merits of nonintervention, then, Hull asked State Department Legal Adviser Green Hackworth to draft a memorandum explaining that even if Roosevelt wished to use the discretionary powers contained in the neutrality law, the ban on arms sales contained in the Spanish Embargo Act of January 8, 1937, would remain in force unless Congress repealed it. Rather than risk a floor fight over what seemed to be a lost cause in Spain at a time when his domestic program was already under fire on Capitol Hill, the president told reporters shortly thereafter that despite his own sympathy for the Spanish Republic, Congress had tied his hands.[61]

Convinced for the first time in almost two years that Roosevelt might be willing to scrap nonintervention, the Loyalist government took steps to persuade American officials that even though the hour was late, the republican cause in Spain was not hopeless. In early April, Foreign Minister Julio Alvarez del Vayo assured Walter Thurston, the American charge d'affaires in Barcelona, that "Loyalist forces are now fighting effectively" and that Prime Minister Juan Negrin would soon reorganize his cabinet to combat "widespread rear guard disaffection." Thurston, however, questioned whether "the reorganization of the Government itself will be especially helpful." Indeed, after anarchist and Communist officials entered a broader coalition cabinet on April 6, he complained that "this development again turns the [Loyalist] Government to the left." A week later William Chapman, the American Consul at Gibraltar, confirmed that the Loyalists were still "bloody Red" and reminded the State Department that "had the Reds won in Spain, the Reds in France would have acted at once," encouraging "Russia to believe it could pierce the heart of Western Europe by thrusting the arrow of communism and anarchy from the Spanish shore of the Mediterranean to the Baltic Sea." Damned by the *Daily Worker* as "Modern Benedict Arnolds," the State Department was in no mood even to consider lifting the Spanish embargo.[62]

With the approach of summer, however, critics of nonintervention stepped up their pressure on the Roosevelt administration to alter its policy in Spain. The Loyalist government, for example, shrewdly employed Breckinridge Long, the former U.S. ambassador to Italy and inveterate anti-Communist, to lobby for the repeal of the Spanish embargo in Washington. Throughout April, Long tried repeatedly to persuade his old State Department associates and congressional leaders that the war in Spain was really a struggle between fascism and democracy, not between bolshevism and nationalism.[63] Raymond Leslie Buell, president of the influential Foreign Policy Association, likewise insisted on April 17 that to deny aid to the Spanish Loyalists any longer would serve only to encourage German and Italian aggression, making wider war more, not less, likely. "Those conservatives who favor discriminating against the Loyalist government out of fear of communism," he added, "fail to realize that such a policy will drive all the weak countries toward Soviet Russia."[64] On May 2, amidst

mounting clamor among like-minded critics on Capitol Hill, North
Dakota Senator Gerald Nye introduced a bill lifting the embargo
on American arms sales to Loyalist Spain, a bill the State Department feared would pass by a wide margin.[65]

With the president vacationing in the Caribbean, Senate Foreign
Relations Committee Chairman Key Pittman asked Cordell Hull
on May 3rd to clarify the Roosevelt administration's position on
the Nye Resolution. Determined to "preserve our neutrality" in
Spain, Hull and his top aides realized that passage of the proposed
legislation virtually guaranteed that Roosevelt would authorize the
sale of arms to the Spanish Loyalists. As a result, a high-ranking
State Department official apparently leaked information about the
impending repeal of the embargo to Arthur Krock on May 4,
something Interior Secretary Ickes angrily labeled "a deliberate
plant in order to stir up the Catholics to protest against its lifting
and thus make it impossible for the President to act."[66] The
following morning, *The New York Times* carried a front page story
that "Roosevelt Backs Lifting Arms Embargo on Spain" and that
"a canvass of the Senate shows that a wide majority will vote for
the Nye Resolution with the Administration supporting it."[67]

The leak had the desired effect. Roosevelt returned from the
Caribbean in early May to face an angry chorus of prominent
Catholic conservatives who, like Postmaster General and Democratic National Committee chairman James Farley, opposed repeal
of the embargo and believed that Franco's rebellion had "saved
Spain from the Communists."[68] Although three-quarters of the
public now sided with the Loyalists, the President was unwilling
to risk alienating so many leading Catholics, and when Hull
forwarded a draft memorandum opposing the Nye Resolution to
the White House on May 10, it was returned with a scrawled "O.K.
FDR." Hull informed Pittman of the Roosevelt administration's
objections two days later and the Senate tabled the bill. When Ickes
complained that Washington's failure to aid Spanish democracy
in its hour of need was "a black page in American history,"
Roosevelt replied "frankly that to raise the embargo would mean
the loss of every Catholic vote next fall."[69]

Shortly after the November 1938 elections, the interior secretary prodded Roosevelt one last time to lift the embargo. Prominent Catholic laymen now favored its repeal, Ickes noted on November 23, in order to impede Hitler's aggression, as did many Latin American liberals, who feared that U.S. nonintervention in Spain might be used as a precedent against them should they face right-wing military revolts.[70] "I agree absolutely with the desirability of a change," Roosevelt replied two days later. But, he added, the State Department was already on record opposing repeal, and his own authority to act under the discretionary clauses of the May 1937 Neutrality Act seemed "rather definitely open to argument." Nevertheless, the President did see "some merit" in Ickes's proposal, and asked Attorney General Homer Cummings for a ruling on November 28. Just before Christmas, however, Cummings sided with the State Department, and the embargo remained in force.[71]

As the war in Spain ground inexorably toward a Franco victory early in the new year, Roosevelt acknowledged that the American policy of nonintervention had probably been an error. When reporters questioned the wisdom of retaining the embargo during a January 24, 1939, press conference, he replied acidly, "You will have to ask the State Department about that."[72] At a cabinet meeting three days later, Roosevelt frankly admitted "for the first time, that the embargo had been a mistake" because it "controverted old American principles and invalidated established international law."[73]

Several officials on the other side of the Atlantic agreed that the anti-Communist underpinnings of nonintervention had blinded the Western democracies to the Fascist threat in Spain. "The first thing that strikes an observer on entering Government Spain is that the epithet 'red' has been vastly over-worked," Ralph S. Stevenson, Britain's new representative in the Loyalist zone, advised Whitehall shortly after arriving in Barcelona in November 1938. "The danger of a communist Spain, if it ever existed," he added two months later, "is a thing of the past." Convinced that Franco's "subservience . . . to one or more of the dictatorial Powers" was a virtual certainty should he emerge victorious, Stevenson urged his superiors on January 15, 1939, to scrap nonintervention, shore up the beleaguered Loyalist regime, and "redress the balance in Spain" with an eye to producing a compromise peace.[74] Diplomatic Adviser Robert Vansittart echoed Stevenson's views in a pithy remark the next day, reminding Foreign Secretary Halifax that "a Franco victory is disastrous to our own interests."[75]

Halifax, however, was less certain that disaster loomed, and consulted Owen O'Malley, Whitehall's chief Southern European specialist, who had recently been sent to St. Jean de Luz to monitor the situation across the border in Spain. Still fearful, as he had been since the autumn of 1936, that "communism might regain control in the event of the Republican Government winning the war," O'Malley urged Whitehall to "waste no time in granting [Franco] recognition."[76] A compromise peace based on "the theory that a mixture of Red and White makes pink," he wrote Halifax on January 24, had "no warrant in the history of Spain." Since a Loyalist defeat was now inevitable, O'Malley concluded that "it seems only common sense that we should, once it is clear that General Franco is master of Spain," extend "prompt and unconditional recognition." Permanent Under Secretary Cadogan agreed, as did the foreign secretary. "What would Dept. anticipate would be probable occasion of recognition," Halifax asked on February 2. "Fall of Madrid?"[77] The occasion came more quickly than Whitehall had anticipated, for after receiving assurances from Franco that he would treat the vanquished Loyalists with "clemency," Halifax was able to persuade the cabinet on February 22 to extend recognition. Even though Madrid remained in Loyalist hands, Britain formally recognized the Franco regime as the legitimate government of Spain on February 27, 1939.[78]

The State Department was as eager as the Foreign Office to grant speedy recognition to Franco, though for slightly different reasons. Convinced that it was "only a question of time until the Loyalist forces . . . surrender," Pierrepont Moffat urged Hull in early February to be mindful of "protecting our vast investment in Franco territory." Well aware that Britain and France were almost certain to establish formal ties with Spain's new caudillo before the month was out, both men worried that American economic interests would suffer if the United States did not follow suit.[79] Claude Bowers, on the other hand, argued that even though it was too late to reverse the outcome in Spain, Roosevelt must not act precipitously, lest recognition be interpreted by the European dictators as further evidence of American pusillanimity. The president agreed, and advised Hull on February 23 that "there need be no haste in recognition of the Franco Government." But Roosevelt also instructed Bowers to return to Washington for consultations, which most friends of republican Spain surely interpreted as a signal that the White House now regarded the Loyalist cause as lost. When Bowers arrived at the Oval Office in early March, the president made no excuses. "We have made a mistake," he confessed. "You have been right all along."[80]

The consequences of that mistake became clearer with each passing week as the Spanish tragedy drew to a close. On March 6 word came that disgruntled Loyalist officers in Madrid had "thrown out Negrin and the Communists" and were "apparently willing to negotiate a military peace with Franco." ITT and other U.S. firms operating in Spain now insisted that Washington must recognize the Franco regime as soon as possible, because "each day's delay is costing American business untold sums."[81] When Madrid fell to Franco's forces on March 28, the White House could no longer postpone a decision. The following morning, Hull conferred with Welles, Dunn, Moffat, and other top State Department officials, who agreed that although Roosevelt himself was still "in no hurry at all," the United States must "recognize the Franco regime in two or three days." This step was necessary, as Moffat put it, "partly because our business interests demand it" and "partly because we and Soviet Russia alone have not recognized the inevitable—an embarrassing partnership." At a second meeting on the 30th, Hull "marshalled his points with a view to persuading the President," and the next day Roosevelt reluctantly agreed to establish diplomatic relations with Franco effective April 1, 1939. "It would have been a mistake," Moffat observed that evening with unintended irony, "to ignore facts."[82]

Indeed, for too long too many British and American policymakers had ignored facts in Spain, focusing on the specter of Communist subversion and ignoring the danger of Fascist aggression. Hull and his top aides, like Halifax and most of the Whitehall bureaucracy, remained as convinced in 1939 as they had been in 1936 that the Spanish Civil War was really a battle between communism and nationalism, and that its outcome was certain to influence European politics as a whole. Both the State Department and the Foreign Office believed that a Loyalist triumph at Madrid would accelerate the spread of bolshevism to Paris, Lisbon, and the other capitals of Europe. A Franco victory, on the other hand, would offer yet another antidote against the Communist contagion and might even persuade Hitler and Mussolini to turn their attention to the alleged source of the epidemic in Moscow.

Not everyone, of course, endorsed this ideological prescription with such zeal. Franklin Roosevelt had long been uncomfortable with the State Department's tendency to equate radical change in Spain with incipient bolshevism, and Anthony Eden had grave doubts about his own anti-Communist assumptions before the Spanish embargo was even six months old. Yet the longer nonintervention remained in force, the more difficult it was to repeal. Roosevelt and Eden might question the wisdom of a policy which sacrificed Spanish democracy at the altar of international fascism, but neither man could overcome the bureaucratic inertia and the ideological myopia which masqueraded as diplomatic wisdom at the State Department and the Foreign Office. The domestic political risks and the international dangers associated with lifting the embargo made it all too easy for Hull and Halifax to persuade their superiors that the benefits of continued neutrality in the Spanish Civil War outweighed the costs. Nonintervention was attractive precisely because it provided the perfect lever to tilt the balance in Spain from left to right at minimal cost to the United States and

Great Britain. That so many high-ranking officials in Washington and London were seduced by its sinister beauty merely confirms the intimate relationship during the late 1930s between antibolshevism and appeasement.

NOTES

1. Accounts which treat nonintervention primarily in the context of military and strategic considerations include Richard P. Traina, *American Diplomacy and the Spanish Civil War* (Bloomington: Indiana University Press, 1968) and Jill Edwards, *The British Government and the Spanish Civil War 1936–1939* (New York: Macmillan, 1979). Works that emphasize the ideological dimension include K. W. Watkins, *Britain Divided: The Effect of the Spanish Civil War on British Political Opinion* (London: Nelson, 1963) and Douglas Little, *Malevolent Neutrality: The United States, Great Britain, and the Origins of the Spanish Civil War* (Ithaca, N.Y.: Cornell University Press, 1985).

2. Little, *Malevolent Neutrality*, chaps. 4–5, passim.

3. Ibid., chaps. 3, 9, passim.

4. Douglas Little, "Twenty Years of Turmoil: ITT, the State Department, and Spain, 1924–1944," *Business History Review* (Winter 1979), pp. 468–69; Little, *Malevolent Neutrality*, pp. 195, 200.

5. Little, *Malevolent Neutrality*, pp. 195–96, 203–4.

6. Long to Hull, October 18, 1935, 765.84/2245, Record Group 59, State Decimal File, National Archives, Washington, D.C. (hereafter cited as NA RG59); Moffat to James Dunn, January 3, 1936, Moffat Papers, Correspondence, vol. 10, Houghton Library, Harvard University.

7. Sir Charles Wingfield (Lisbon) to Eden, March 4, 1936, W2234/478/36; Eden to Wingfield, March 29, 1936, W2676/478/36; and Chilton to Eden, tel. March 25, 1936, and minutes by Evelyn Schuckburgh and Horace Seymour, March 27, 1936, W2677/478/36, FO371, General Correspondence of the Foreign Office, 1910–1945, Public Record Office, Kew, Surrey, England (hereafter cited as PRO FO371).

8. MacVeagh to FDR, June 13, 1936, in Edgar B. Nixon, ed., *Franklin Roosevelt and Foreign Affairs 1933–36*, 3 vols. (Cambridge, Mass.: Belknap Press of Harvard University Press, 1969), vol. 3, pp. 319–23 (hereafter cited as *FDR & Foreign Affairs 1933–36*); John S. Koliopoulos, *Greece and the British Connection 1935–1941* (New York: Clarendon Press, 1977), pp. 38–59; George Mavrogordatos, *Stillborn Republic: Social Conditions and Party Strategies in*

Greece 1922–1936 (Berkeley: University of California Press, 1983), pp. 345–49.

9. Long to Phillips, March 20, 1936, Phillips Papers, Memoranda of Conversations as Under Secretary of State 1935 [sic], vol. 36, Houghton Library, Harvard University; Straus to FDR, May 13 and 15, 1936, and Straus to Hull, May 14, 1936, *FDR & Foreign Affairs 1933–36*, vol. 3, pp. 300–4; and FDR to Straus, June 8, 1936, in Elliott Roosevelt, ed., *FDR: His Personal Letters 1928–1945*, 2 vols. (New York: Duell, Sloan and Pearce, 1950), vol. 1, pp. 593–94 (hereafter cited as *FDR Personal Letters*).

10. Vansittart to Clerk, June 10, 1936, C4238/1/17; Clerk to Vansittart, June 11, 1936, C4355/1/17; Clerk to Eden, tel. June 15, 1936, minute by Sargent, June 17, 1936, and undated minute by Eden, C4319/1/17, PRO FO371, vols. 19857 and 19858.

11. Little, *Malevolent Neutrality*, pp. 205–8.

12. Bowers to Hull, June 3, 1936, and undated memorandum by Dunn, 852.00/2170, NA RG59; memorandum by William Montagu Pollock, June 23, 1936, and Vansittart to Eden, June 24, 1936 W5693/62/41, PRO FO371, vol. 20522.

13. Little, *Malevolent Neutrality*, pp. 226–27, 232–33.

14. Ibid., pp. 223–24, 233–38.

15. Memorandum by Sargent, August 12, 1936, and minute by Cadogan, August 13, 1936, W9331/62/41, PRO FO371, vol. 20534.

16. Little, *Malevolent Neutrality*, pp. 245–46.

17. Minute by Eden, August 20, 1936, C5939/1/17, PRO FO371, vol. 19858.

18. Minute by Gladwyn Jebb, November 25, 1936, W15925/4719/41, PRO FO371, vol. 20570; Vansittart, "The World Situation and British Rearmament," December 31, 1936, in Great Britain, Foreign Office, *Documents on British Foreign Policy 1919–1939*, 2nd series, 19 vols. (H.M. Stationery Office, 1946–1982), vol. 17, pp. 779–80.

19. Dante Puzzo, *Spain and the Great Powers 1936–1941* (New York: Columbia University Press, 1962), pp. 141–48; Gabriel Jackson, *The Spanish Republic and the Civil War, 1931–1939* (Princeton, N.J.: Princeton University Press, 1965), pp. 317–20; T. G. Powell, "Mexico," in Mark Falcoff and Frederick Pike, eds., *The Spanish Civil War: American Hemispheric Perspectives* (Lincoln: University of Nebraska Press, 1982), pp. 54–73.

20. Kelley to Joseph Green, December 3, 1936, "Spain—Memoranda 1936," Box 13, Joseph Green Papers, Seeley G. Mudd Library, Princeton University, Princeton, N.J.

21. Moore to Bullitt (Paris), December 29, 1936, *Foreign Relations of the United States: Diplomatic Papers, 1936*, vol. 2, pp. 618–19 (hereafter cited as *FRUS*); Wayne S. Cole, *Roosevelt and the Isolationists 1932–45* (Lincoln: University of Nebraska Press, 1983), pp. 225–26; Traina, *American Diplomacy and the Spanish Civil War*, pp. 81–84.

22. Telegrams from Thomas and Einstein and an undated letter from Greig are all in "Spanish Civil War—January–June 1937," OF 422C, Franklin D. Roosevelt Library (hereafter known as FDRL).
23. Green to John H. Morgan, January 17, 1944, "Miscellaneous Spain Documents," Box 13, Green Papers. Green and Morgan were at work on a State Department "White Paper" on the Spanish Civil War throughout 1944.
24. Little, *Malevolent Neutrality*, pp. 249, 257, 263.
25. Bowers, Diary, December 1 and 14, 1936, Claude G. Bowers Papers, Lilly Library, Indiana University, Bloomington, Ind.; William R. Castle Diary, December 11, 1936, Houghton Library, Harvard University, Cambridge, Mass.
26. Krock Memoranda, n.d. [early 1937], Book I 1928–1948, p. 82a, Arthur Krock Papers, Seeley G. Mudd Library, Princeton University, Princeton, N.J.
27. Phillips to FDR, January 14, 1937, Official File 2314, FDR Presidential Library, Hyde Park, N.Y.; FDR to Phillips, February 6, 1937, *FDR Personal Letters*, vol. 1, p. 656.
28. Harold Ickes, *The Secret Diary of Harold L. Ickes, Vol. 2: The Inside Struggle 1936–1939* (New York: Simon and Schuster, 1954), p. 93.
29. Allen S. Everest, *Morgenthau, the New Deal, and Silver* (New York: King's Crown Press, 1950), p. 126; William Leuchtenburg, *Franklin D. Roosevelt and the New Deal 1932–1940* (New York: Harper and Row, 1963), p. 223.
30. Traina, *American Diplomacy and Spanish Civil War*, pp. 108–11.
31. R. Walton Moore to Bowers, March 17, 1937, and Bowers to Moore, March 29, 1937, both in Box 3, R. Walton Moore Papers, FDRL.
32. Hull Memorandum, June 7, 1937, Reel 32, Cordell Hull Papers (microfilm edition), Library of Congress, Washington, D.C.
33. Douglas Little, "Claude Bowers and His Mission to Spain," in K. Paul Jones, ed., *U.S. Diplomats in Europe, 1919–1941* (Santa Barbara, Calif.: ABC-Clio, 1981), pp. 141–43; Bowers to FDR, February 16, 1937, in Donald B. Schewe, ed., *FDR & Foreign Affairs 1937–39*, 13 vols. (New York: Garland Press, 1979), vol. 4, pp. 186–90 (hereafter cited as *FDR & Foreign Affairs 1937–39*); Bowers Diary, June 24, 1937, Bowers Papers, Lilly Library, Indiana University, Bloomington, Ind.
34. Cole, *Roosevelt and the Isolationists*, pp. 229–30; FDR to Hull, June 29, 1937, President's Secretary's File (PSF), Box 11 ("Neutrality"), FDRL.
35. Phillips to FDR, April 22, 1937, *FDR & Foreign Affairs 1937–39*, vol. 5, pp. 91–95.
36. Bingham to Hull, tel. July 6, 1937, *FRUS, 1937*, vol. 1, pp. 353–55; Eden to Ambassador Ronald Lindsay (Washington), July 6, 1937, "Sp/37/4," the Papers of Lord Avon [Anthony Eden], Record Group FO954, Public Record Office, Kew, England.
37. Minutes of Cabinet Meeting, January 8, 1937, vol. 360, Record Group PREM 1, Records of the Prime Minister's Office, Public Record Office, Kew, England.

38. Stimson Diary, January 4, 1937, Reel 5, Microfilm Edition.

39. Perkins to Hull, February 3, 1937, 852.00/4771, NA RG59.

40. Bowers to Hull, February 23, 1937, General Correspondence, Bowers Papers.

41. Chatfield to Roger Backhouse, February 16, 1937, quoted in Lawrence Pratt, *East of Malta, West of Suez: Britain's Mediterranean Crisis 1936–1939* (New York: Cambridge University Press, 1975), pp. 43–44.

42. K. W. Watkins, *Britain Divided: The Effect of the Spanish Civil War on British Political Opinion* (London: Nelson, 1963), pp. 163–82; Bill Alexander, *British Volunteers for Liberty: Spain 1936–1939* (London: Lawrence and Wishart, 1982), pp. 91–97.

43. Samuel Hoare, "Admiralty Spring 1937," Folder 3, Box 9; and Hoare to Chamberlain, March 17, 1937, Folder 2, Box 9, both in Templewood [Hoare] Papers, Cambridge University Library, Cambridge, England.

44. Herschel V. Johnson (London) to Hull, August 23, 1937; and Robert T. Pell to Pierrepont Moffat, September 8, 1937, both in 852.00/6376, NA RG59.

45. Memorandum by Eden, September 7, 1937; and Report of the Second Plenary Meeting of the Nyon Conference, September 14, 1937, both in *Documents on British Foreign Policy*, 2nd series, vol. 19, pp. 245–46, 294–98 (hereafter cited as *DBFP*).

46. Hugh Lloyd Thomas (Paris) to Eden, September 23, 1937; and minute by Vansittart, September 30, 1937, both in W17863/7/41, PRO FO371, vol. 21365.

47. Eden quoted in minute by Private Secretary Clifford J. Norton, September 28, 1937; minute by Walter Roberts, September 27, 1937; and minute by Sargent, September 29, 1937, all in W17863/7/41, PRO FO371, vol. 21365.

48. Cabinet Conclusions, October 13, 1937, *DBFP*, 2nd series, vol. 19, pp. 399–403.

49. Ibid.

50. Sargent to Eric Phipps (Rome), October 8 and 15, 1937, Phipps Papers, "Correspondence—1937," vol. 2, Churchill College Library, Cambridge, England.

51. Eden's suggestion is in "Record of conversations between British and French Ministers, November 29 and 30, 1937," *DBFP*, 2nd series, vol. 19, pp. 606, 613–15. Cadogan's views are in a minute dated December 7, 1937, C95/95/62, PRO FO371, vol. 21626.

52. Norman Rose, *Vansittart: Study of a Diplomat* (New York: Holmes and Meier, 1978), pp. 206–14; David Carlton, *Anthony Eden: A Biography* (London: Allen Lane, 1981), pp. 120–31.

53. Minute by Cadogan, March 17, 1938, and Halifax to Soviet ambassador Ivan Maisky, March 24, 1938, C1935/95/62; minutes by Vansittart, June 27, 1938, and by Halifax, July 20, 1938, W8723/29/41, PRO FO371, vols. 21626 and 22627.

54. Moffat, Diplomatic Journal, September 10, 1937, vol. 39, Moffat Papers.

55. "Outcome of Civil War," August 8, 1937, 890 Spain, Record Group 151, Records of the Bureau of Foreign and Domestic Commerce, National Archives, Washington, D.C.

56. Moffat memorandum, January 15, 1938, 852.00/7222, NA RG59.

57. Bowers to FDR, February 20, 1938, and FDR to Bowers, March 7, 1938, *FDR & Foreign Affairs 1937–39*, vol. 8, pp. 340–45, and vol. 9, p. 65; Moffat Diary, March 12, 1938.

58. Moffat Diary, March 12 and 14, 1938.

59. Moffat Diary, April 14, 1938; R. Walton Moore to Hull, May 5, 1938, Box 19, Moore Papers, FDRL; Hull, Draft Memoirs, July 31, and August 19, 1946, Reel 40, Cordell Hull Papers (microfilm edition), Library of Congress, Washington, D.C.; Max Lerner, "Behind Hull's Embargo," *The Nation*, May 28, 1938, pp. 607–10; Leo V. Kanawada, Jr., *Franklin D. Roosevelt's Diplomacy and American Catholics, Italians, and Jews* (Ann Arbor, Mich.: UMI Research Press, 1982), pp. 54–55.

60. Ickes, *Secret Diary*, vol. 2, pp. 377–78.

61. Moffat Diary, March 31, 1938; memorandum by Hackworth, March 31, 1938, and minutes of White House Press Conference, April 28, 1938, both in *FDR & Foreign Affairs 1937–39*, vol. 9, pp. 281–87, 449–53.

62. Thurston to Hull, tels. April 3 and 6, 1938, *FRUS, 1938*, vol. 1, pp. 171–73, 174; Chapman to Hull, April 13, 1938, 852.00/7802, NA RG59; Moffat Diary, April 14, 1938.

63. Kanawada, *Roosevelt's Diplomacy and American Catholics*, pp. 55–59.

64. Buell, letter to the editor, *The New York Times*, April 17, 1938.

65. Moffat Diary, May 3 and 4, 1938.

66. Moffat Diary, May 5, 1938; Ickes, *Secret Diary*, vol. 2, pp. 388–89; Kanawada, *Roosevelt's Diplomacy and American Catholics*, pp. 62–64. Hugh Thomas, *The Spanish Civil War* (New York: Harper and Row, 1977), p. 825, n. 1, notes: "Arthur Krock told me (January 9, 1963) that, so far as he could recall, Hull or Welles gave him the information on which he based this article."

67. *The New York Times*, May 5, 1938.

68. Robert Divine, *The Illusion of Neutrality* (Chicago: University of Chicago Press, 1962), pp. 224–25; Kanawada, *Roosevelt's Diplomacy and American Catholics*, pp. 66–68 (Farley quoted on p. 66).

69. Hull to FDR, May 10, 1938, *FDR & Foreign Affairs 1937–39*, vol. 10, p. 70; Hull to Pittman, May 12, 1938, *FRUS, 1938*, vol. 1, pp. 194–95; Ickes, *Secret Diary*, vol. 2, pp. 389–90.

70. Ickes to FDR, November 23, 1938, *FDR & Foreign Affairs 1937–39*, vol. 12, pp. 161–62.

71. Hull to FDR, November 18, 1938; FDR to Ickes, November 25, 1938; FDR to Cummings, November 28, 1938; Cummings to FDR, December 19,

1938, all in *FDR & Foreign Affairs 1937–39*, vol. 12, pp. 120, 182–83, 196, 340.

72. Transcript of Press Conference, January 24, 1939, ibid., vol. 13, pp. 171–72.

73. FDR quoted in Ickes, *Secret Diary*, vol. 2, p. 569.

74. Stevenson to Halifax, November 25, 1938, W16041/29/41; and Stevenson to Halifax, January 15, 1939, W1081/8/41, PRO FO371, vols. 22631 and 24115.

75. Minute by Vansittart, January 16, 1939, W973/5/41, PRO FO371, vol. 24115.

76. O'Malley quoted in minute by Pollock, January 26, 1939, W1081/8/41, PRO FO371, vol. 24115.

77. O'Malley to Halifax, January 24, 1939; and minutes by Cadogan, February 1, 1939, and Halifax, February 2, 1939, W1615/8/41, PRO FO371, vol. 24115.

78. Edwards, *British Government and Spanish Civil War, pp. 207–10*.

79. Moffat, Diary, February 4 and 5, 1939; Bullitt (Paris) to Hull, tel. February 8, 1939; and Herschel Johnson (London) to Hull, tel. February 14, 1939, *FRUS, 1939*, vol. 2, pp. 740–42, 744–45.

80. Bowers to FDR, February 8 and 16, 1939; Hull to FDR, tel. February 23, 1939; and FDR to Hull, tel. February 23, 1939, *FDR & Foreign Affairs 1937–39*, vol. 13, pp. 266–71, 328, 356, 357; Claude Bowers, *My Mission to Spain* (New York: Simon and Schuster, 1954), p. 418.

81. Moffat Diary, March 6 and 9, 1939.

82. Moffat Diary, March 28, 29, 30, and 31, and April 1, 1939.

3

Munich and American Appeasement

Jane Karoline Vieth

Munich—an evocative word unalterably fixed in our vocabulary—
is synonymous with a provocative foreign policy. To its opponents
the Munich Pact was a dishonorable sell-out to Adolf Hitler's
bullying. To its later defenders it was a shrewd, calculated policy
essential to Britain's security—a policy that bought precious time
for rearming. Signed on September 30, 1938, by Great Britain,
Germany, Italy, and France, the pact required Czechoslovakia to
cede the Sudetenland to Germany. It was an essential element in
Prime Minister Neville Chamberlain's policy of appeasement and
was meant by him to lay the groundwork for a more general
agreement with Germany designed to reduce international tensions
and lead to peace. Even as the ink dried on the pact, a debate arose,
and continues to the present, over whether Munich was necessary
and what was gained by it.[1]

The debate over Chamberlain's foreign policy continues among
historians. The orthodox school accepts the thesis that at the very
least Hitler intended to acquire hegemony in Europe and that
World War II was the direct result of his decision to use military
force. A corollary to this thesis is that Britain, under Chamberlain's
leadership, adopted a deliberate policy of appeasing Germany by
granting concessions to placate Hitler and reduce his ambitions.
The policy of appeasement had its historical origins at least as far

back as World War I. The appeasers pursued colonial and economic concessions actively during the *Anschluss* in March 1938,
with the Munich Pact in September 1938, and throughout the first
half of 1939. Even after Germany's occupation of Prague and
Chamberlain's right-about-face over Prague in March 1939, Britain continued its appeasement policy through nondiplomatic channels. And even after the Polish invasion in September 1939,
appeasement continued in other forms. As long as he remained in
office, until May 1940, Chamberlain hoped for a "compromise
peace."

Critics of this orthodox view argue that World War II could have
been prevented had Hitler's aggression been directly confronted
and challenged by a determined Britain supported by a vigorous
France, among other powers. Somewhere, between Germany's
announcement of rearmament in 1935 and the Polish invasion in
1939, it would have been possible to stop Hitler, critics argue. Two
of the most likely opportunities were the reoccupation of the
Rhineland in March 1936 and the height of the Czech crisis at
Munich in September 1938. Both opportunities were lost, however, and the Nazi war machine kept on rolling until finally Hitler's
weak and unwilling adversaries were forced into war. The policy
of appeasement never had a chance of success.

A major challenger to these two interpretations is A.J.P. Taylor,
who argued that Hitler was really a traditional, shrewd German
statesman pursuing an opportunistic foreign policy for Germany.[2]
If this were so—if Hitler were a consummate chess player busily
checkmating his adversaries—then appeasement should not be
dismissed outright, but missed opportunities criticized, and moves
that failed to retard the chancellor's advance pointed out. Since
Hitler was both a fanatic and a cynical opportunistic, the orthodox
view is more compelling.

The current historiography on British appeasement suggests that
it was not a "coward's creed advanced alone by stupid men,"[3] but
a sensible policy, particularly with respect to colonies and economics. Its error lay in the fact that its advocates did not alter or abandon
it when it became clear that it had failed. Appeasement might be

considered a defensible policy even at Munich, especially considering Britain's inadequate military defenses, but to continue its application after Munich was foolhardy and a disservice to the British. It is argued, further, that appeasement was not the cause of Hitler's expansion or of the outbreak of World War II, something he was determined to have. What another policy might have done was to force Hitler to pursue his ambitions in a less advantageous military position and perhaps make war less appealing. Perhaps a different policy or an earlier appeasement program might have united Britain and the Commonwealth and educated and prepared the British people to meet the scourge of war.

Throughout these negotiations the American government followed a policy of detached observation. President Franklin Roosevelt was walking a tightrope, neither rejecting nor inhibiting appeasement. Bowing to the prevailing national need for a passive foreign policy and fearful that a more aggressive stance could weaken his leadership in domestic affairs, FDR was reduced to making fruitless symbolic gestures and issuing statements in opposition to aggression.[4] In practice the foreign policies of the United States and Great Britain reinforced each other and made them unintentional but undeniable allies. Although America's isolationism denied Britain the material resources necessary for making appeasement a success, the policy of appeasement allowed Americans the luxury of believing that a more active foreign policy was unnecessary.[5] America's diplomatic indebtedness to the appeasement policy was something that the ambassador at the Court of St. James, Joseph P. Kennedy, may not have realized.

Joseph Kennedy—Roosevelt's tart-tongued, freckle-faced, headstrong, mercurial ambassador—only seldom followed Washington's lead. Despite his oft-proclaimed advocacy of American isolation, he undermined Roosevelt's efforts to maintain America's distance by trying to get his government's support for Chamberlain's appeasement policy, to which Kennedy was unswervingly loyal, and by pursuing his own foreign policy initiatives that contravened Washington's official stance of detachment. Receiving little direction from Washington, Kennedy, inexperienced in diplomacy and ill-disposed to listen to advice from subordinates, relied upon his own wits and convictions and was extremely susceptible to the fears and attitudes of his host government. Given his lack of training and experience in international affairs and his proclivity for seeing diplomatic events in personal terms, Kennedy's diplomatic role began as an annoying hindrance and became an embarrassing disaster to Roosevelt and eventually led to a major split between the two.[6]

In this chapter I will describe the events leading up to the Munich Pact and examine them from the perspective of American and British foreign policy as defined by President Roosevelt and Prime Minister Neville Chamberlain. I will focus particularly on the contradictory personal diplomacy of Joseph Kennedy and his diplomatic circumvention and contravention of official policy, and discuss the effect this had on his relationship with Roosevelt. I will also mention the impact of Munich on the subsequent formation of foreign policy in both the United States and Britain, and I will review some of the historical debate about Munich and its myth.

Joseph Kennedy, the new American ambassador, had barely unpacked his bags and become familiar with embassy routine when he faced his first major diplomatic crisis. On March 12, 1938, Hitler's troops rolled across the border into Austria and incorporated the Republic into the Third Reich. Hitler predicted: "This will be very inconvenient to the Czechs."[7] The *Anschluss* foreshadowed the tragic drama over Czechoslovakia that was played out throughout the spring and summer of 1938. That lizard-shaped, elongated kidney, that polyglot nation of "Czecho-Germano-Polano-Magyaro-Rutheno-Roumano-Slovakia,"[8] as Mussolini called it, once part of the now defunct Austro-Hungarian Empire, was a state of diverse and seldom harmonious nationalities; in addition to the 3.5 million Germans in the Sudetenland, there were 7.5 million Czechs, 2.3 million Slovaks, and smaller numbers of Magyars, Ruthenians, and Poles.[9] Doomed by geography and politics, it was landlocked, strategically located in Central Europe, easy to strangle economically, militarily outflanked, and surrounded by a sea of hostile neighbors: Germany, Poland, Rumania, and Hungary. The Sudeten Germans, closely tied to their Austrian cousins racially and historically, provided a convenient pretext for Hitler's ambitions. He demanded the end of "oppression" and urged "self-determination" for the 3.5 million "brothers" living under Czech rule—a policy that would ensure the annexation of the Sudetenland to Germany and the destruction of the Czech Republic. Its elimination would not only destroy a potential Russian or Anglo-French military base, but also give him Czechoslovakia's rich natural resources, its industrial capacity, and the undisputed hegemony of Central Europe.

Both France and Britain were keenly aware of many of Hitler's ambitions and wanted to avert a crisis and preserve peace. The French had an explicit obligation to aid the Czechs under the terms of their 1925 mutual-defense treaty and a 1935 alliance with the Soviet Union. The British had only a vague commitment to the Czechs as fellow members of the wobbly League of Nations and an obligation under the still-valid 1925 Locarno Agreement to aid France if she were the victim of unprovoked aggression.

Addressing the House of Commons on March 24, Chamberlain set the policy his government would follow throughout the remainder of 1938. While he promised to defend Britain's traditional commitments, the prime minister said that the basis of Britain's foreign policy, "the maintenance and preservation of peace," remained unchanged. In discussing the central question of the German minorities in Czechoslovakia and what Britain's relationship to them should be, Chamberlain made an equivocal statement constantly quoted throughout the tense summer months: "Where peace and war are concerned, legal obligations are not alone involved, and if war broke out, it would be unlikely to be confined to those who have assumed such obligations. It would be quite impossible to say where it would end and what Governments might become involved."[10] Thus the prime minister's diplomatic agenda for the next months was to make no further commitments to Czechoslovakia and to encourage both Berlin and Prague to reach an internal Czech settlement.

Perhaps reassured by Chamberlain's promise not to make further Czech commitments, Kennedy told the American Club of London the next day that there would be no war in 1938.[11]

Even in the early months of the Czech crisis the ever-faithful Kennedy stood by Chamberlain, serving as his loyal confidant and dutiful reporter to the American government. Lord Halifax, Britain's foreign secretary, had promised him that he would receive confidential information and be kept fully informed of "all British movements of importance."[12] The foreign secretary kept his word. Not only had Kennedy been briefed beforehand about the prime minister's March 24 parliamentary statement, but throughout the crisis he was privy to Chamberlain's decisions. The ambassador did such a thorough job of informing Washington that Sumner Welles at the State Department later praised him. "I can't tell you how admirably you have been keeping us informed. It couldn't be better."[13]

Concern among British officials over Czechoslovakia reached fever pitch during the May crisis and nearly destroyed Chamberlain's hopes for a peaceful solution. Negotiations between Konrad Henlein, the pro-Nazi leader of the Sudeten Germans, and Eduard Benes, the president of the Prague government, broke down over Sudeten German demands. Rumors of panic and troop movements reached London as a lightning German assault appeared imminent. London warned against precipitous action, and Halifax informed the German ambassador that if the Czechs were attacked and France upheld her treaty obligations, then Britain might enter the conflict. Hitler met with his advisers on May 28, and in his May 30 directive, set October 1 as the deadline for the invasion of Czechoslovakia. The crisis passed. There was no coup.

The only important act by the American government during the early stages of the Czech crisis was the release of Secretary of State Cordell Hull's press statement of May 28, 1938. The United States, Hull said, considered the Central European situation "critical" and had followed the recent events with "close and anxious attention."[14]

Kennedy complacently watched the Czech crisis unfold. His detailed dispatches throughout the spring had nothing of the passionate hysterical tone they later acquired. He saw the crisis largely through the eyes of his host and agreed with Chamberlain's position that Britain's military weakness spelled certain defeat. Years later Kennedy told a friend that Chamberlain's attitude throughout 1938 was that Britain "had nothing with which to fight and that she could not risk going to war with Hitler."[15] The ambassador was quite critical of Britain's jingoes and of "warmongers" like Winston Churchill, whom he accused of urging war on an unprepared Britain. He was determined from the outset that if war came, the United States would keep out of the conflict.[16] Thus his position was set and remained constant until the outbreak of war: support the appeasement policy for Britain and maintain American isolation.

Kennedy's initial analysis of the Czech situation proved to be shortsighted. He was well informed, but he did not cultivate other "unofficial" channels of information or develop a compatible professional relationship with sources critical of the Chamberlain government such as Anthony Eden, Halifax's predecessor at the Foreign Office, or Winston Churchill, who better understood the aggressive nature of nazism.

Despite his approval of FDR's performance as a "detailed observer," and of Chamberlain's Czechoslovakia policy of "no further commitments," Kennedy had become plainly worried by spring. Roosevelt's secretary of the interior, Harold Ickes, honeymooning in London, visited him and sympathetically listened to him rail. "Joe Kennedy was full of the European situation. He was greatly afraid that hell might break loose at any time over Czechoslovakia." He intended to tell Roosevelt about it as soon as he got home. The frightened ambassador left no doubt in his visitor's mind "that he was very nervous over the entire European situation."[17]

Kennedy's nervousness grew from his almost complete disavowal of war as the ultimate weapon in the statesman's arsenal. He was motivated by economic self-interest as well as other personal reasons. He thought that war was "irrational and debasing." War destroys capitalism. What could be worse than that? "I have four boys," he once said, "and I don't want them to be killed in a foreign war."[18]

Kennedy's fear of war led him to gamble on a more perilous brand of personal diplomacy that ironically could have weakened both appeasement and isolationism. At a time when most other diplomats were busily dissociating American foreign policy from Europe's affairs, Kennedy quietly initiated a series of conversations with Herbert von Dirksen, the German ambassador in London during the summer of 1938. No evidence suggests that Kennedy was acting with administrative approval or foreknowledge.[19] According to von Dirksen's report to the German foreign minister, he and the American ambassador discussed a wide range of issues during their first meeting on June 13: Germany's "Jewish question" and Kennedy's suggestion that Germany make less clamor over it, Germany's position in Europe, and Germany's relations with the United States, among other topics. Kennedy told von Dirksen that he intended to leave shortly for a nine-day visit in the United States. The American ambassador wanted to give the president a full report about conditions in Europe and to urge that "above all" the United States should "establish friendly relations with Germany." In fact, he assured the German ambassador, "the President was not anti-German" and the vast majority of American people also wanted "peace and friendly relations with Germany." The anti-German sentiment was primarily concentrated on the East Coast where most of the 3.5 million Jews lived. Von Dirksen criticized the "poisonous role" of the press and appealed to Kennedy to use his influence with the government and with the president in particular to persuade the press to speak more favorably of Germany. For his part, Kennedy believed that the present German government "had done great things for Germany" because "the Germans were satisfied and enjoyed good living conditions." He also approved of Germany's economic expansion in the east and the southeast. On the basis of their first conversation, von Dirksen rejected any thought that Kennedy was operating from personal political motives and reported to the German Foreign Ministry that he had a "good impression of Mr. Kennedy."[20]

Upon Kennedy's return to England, the two foreign ambassadors met again on July 20 for a "spirited and interesting" conver-

sation. Kennedy was concerned about the economic problems in
the United States and in the world economy that remained un-
solved. He also told von Dirksen that American opinion of Germany had "deteriorated appreciably." The average American held
Germany responsible for the general worldwide economic insecur-
ity and accused it of wanting to provoke war, Kennedy told him.
Furthermore, he reportedly said, Roosevelt was willing to support
"any efforts to promote general tranquillity and create favorable
economic conditions" and he would "support Germany's demands
vis-à-vis England or . . . do anything that might lead to pacification."
    The German ambassador concluded that it was obvious that the
United States saw itself as the "protector and helper of England,"
who in turn owed "subservience and obedience" to the United
States. Roosevelt's administration not only "supports the Chamberlain Cabinet," he concluded, but "assists it in overcoming all
difficulties," including undermining his opposition by supporting
Chamberlain's desire for a settlement with Germany—statements
to which Roosevelt would have taken great exception. Kennedy
was "much more worried and pessimistic" than he had previously
been, von Dirksen reported to the German Foreign Ministry. "The
idea that Germany might go to war against Czechoslovakia, which
would then result in the intervention of England and France and,
first indirectly and then directly, of the United States, appeared to
have a pretty firm hold on him." On the basis of their conversation,
the German ambassador concluded that Kennedy was "acting on
orders from Roosevelt," who needed successes in the economic
field for the upcoming election.[21] Although there is no evidence
to suggest that Kennedy was acting under Roosevelt's orders, he
probably did accurately assess Kennedy's motive, believing him
"sincere in his efforts to create a better atmosphere in German-
American relations."[22] In addition, Kennedy may also have believed that his personal diplomatic initiative was necessary because
Roosevelt was misinformed and unaware of the seriousness of the
situation in Europe—something for which he blamed "the career
boys" in the State Department.
    Kennedy's personal diplomatic initiative with von Dirksen pro-

duced ambiguous results. On the one hand, he demonstrated professional diplomatic skills by cultivating a pleasant relationship with von Dirksen, who stated that he found Kennedy's gestures believable and sincere. Furthermore, if von Dirksen's account is an accurate reflection of his conversation with Kennedy, then perhaps the American diplomat, who always liked to be liked, did mean to flatter the Nazi regime by his pro-German remarks and his seeming sympathy over the "Jewish question." On the other hand, the judgment of a diplomat who expresses himself willing to sacrifice the Jews or the Czechs in order to preserve peace is extremely suspect. Kennedy's role as ambassador was to describe and report facts accurately, not to circumvent the administration and try to initiate policy on his own authority.

In addition to initiating the von Dirksen conversations, Kennedy also tried to get FDR publicly to endorse the Runciman mission. By mid-July the negotiations between Czechoslovakia and the Sudeten Germans had broken down, and Chamberlain decided to send Lord Runciman to Germany. He was to mediate between the two parties, to listen to their arguments and facts, and to suggest modifications in their positions. Runciman's efforts were ultimately unsuccessful, and the diplomatic standoff between Henlein and Benes in Czechoslovakia continued.

Before making the surprise announcement to the House of Commons about the mission on July 23, Chamberlain informed Kennedy of his intentions. The ambassador reported to Hull that Chamberlain had told him that the situation with Germany was improved and that he hoped that the Czechoslovakian matter "will be adjusted without difficulty and that . . . they will start negotiations with Germany."[23] He also dutifully passed on to the State Department the request by Halifax "that should the President or the Secretary feel that he could make some public statement expressing approval of Lord Runciman's mission this would have a favorable effect on world opinion and Lord Halifax would naturally be much gratified."[24] The president, however, was on vacation and hard to reach. When he returned to Washington he decided to continue his policy of silence awhile longer. Roosevelt turned a deaf ear.

Kennedy tried another approach. During an hour-long conversation in late August, an anxious Chamberlain worried out loud to him and surprised him with the news that there was a 50-50 chance of war since Hitler intended to have Czechoslovakia one way or another. "My own impression," Kennedy assured the State Department, was that Chamberlain would use his influence to keep France and Britain out of war. When Kennedy asked Chamberlain whether or not he would join France if war broke out, Chamberlain replied that he "might be forced into it." "It will be hell," replied Kennedy.

Upset by the war of nerves and worried about the possibility of a general European war, the ambassador realized that the isolationist position of the United States would be extremely difficult to maintain. If France and Britain entered the war, "the United States would follow before long," he predicted to Chamberlain. "We were not, however, in a position to stop Hitler," Chamberlain replied. "In the circumstances it would be unwise to utter threats." Kennedy loyally told him that this was the right position to adopt.[25] He then asked the prime minister whether there was anything that the U.S. government might do. Chamberlain, who did not believe that Americans could deliver anything but words, said no. Despite this refusal, an excited Kennedy, apparently without consulting Washington, next offered Chamberlain a blank check. Giving him a sweeping assurance of support, Kennedy stated that he believed that the president had intended "to go in with Chamberlain; whatever course Chamberlain decided to adopt I would think right." Further, the ambassador added, if the prime minister wanted FDR to "do anything," then he "would be glad to know about it."[26] Thus, the American ambassador conveyed a totally erroneous sense of approval and enthusiasm on FDR's part and apparently meant that the president would accept anything ranging from a sell-out of the Czechs to war with Germany. Further, it was a promise diametrically opposed to Kennedy's oft-repeated isolationist position and in contravention to Washington's official stance. Apparently Kennedy failed to see that such a sweeping gesture without guarantees of American diplomatic or military support was meaningless and contrary to his desire to maintain American isolation from Europe's affairs.

The next day, however, Kennedy rescinded his impetuous offer of a blank check. He gave Halifax a more circumscribed view of American intentions. While the United States would be "shocked" by German aggression, Kennedy told the British foreign secretary, he did not think it would be necessary for Britain to go to war over Germany's aggression.[27] Chamberlain no doubt realized that Kennedy's enthusiastic offer of a blank check was not a solid basis on which to establish a policy of bluff and that Kennedy was not always an accurate or reliable spokesman for the administration. While Kennedy was telling Hull that Chamberlain was still the "best bet" in Europe today against war, the prime minister was telling his cabinet that American foreign policy was that of the "mugwump."[28] His strategy continued to be to respond to the Czech crisis without much concern for the United States. Thus in the last days of August, Kennedy was still optimistic about peace, quite willing to cooperate with Chamberlain and to support his appeasement policy so long as it maintained peace, and willing to urge the Roosevelt Administration to do so too, apparently with or without its prior approval.

Kennedy again interceded with Washington on Britain's behalf. In late summer, the ambassador, prompted by Halifax, pressed Washington to elaborate on its foreign policy stance. What would America's reaction be if Germany invaded Czechoslovakia and Britain did not fight? Halifax asked Kennedy nearly a month before Munich. Kennedy turned to the secretary of state for advice. "I think that the Prime Minister and the Foreign Secretary would appreciate your reaction and judgment, so far as the United States goes, as to what should be done on this."[29]

Hull's stiff and noncommittal response on September 1 to Kennedy's request for more guidance referred the ambassador to the recent public speeches of administration officials, which were prepared "with great care" and which "accurately reflect the attitude of this Government and world situation."[30] In an August 16 radio address the secretary had warned the Axis nations that "our own situation is profoundly affected by what happens elsewhere in the world," and two days later on August 18 at Kingston, Ontario, Roosevelt inserted into the State Department's text the promise that "the people of the United States will not stand idly by if domination of Canadian soil is threatened by any other empire."[31] Beyond expressing a vague interest in events outside the hemisphere, the Administration would not go. Hull told Kennedy that it would not be "practicable to be more specific as to our reaction in hypothetical circumstances."[32] Kennedy may have gotten the message. When Halifax later asked again, "What would America do?" Kennedy's response was: "I had not the slightest idea except that we want to keep out of war."[33]

The secretary accused Kennedy of pursuing his own private foreign policies and starting the rumor of a London-Paris-Washington peace axis. Hull feared the resulting embarrassment to the United States if Britain and France were to go to war. Kennedy's "personal diplomacy," his diplomatic circumvention and contravention of official policy, scared the administration into believing that it had become a party to the British game either way. "Kennedy is playing with the British Foreign Office and the Prime Minister. He has spilled the beans, and the President knows that,"[34] wrote Henry Morgenthau, Jr., Roosevelt's confidant and treasury secretary.

Roosevelt and Kennedy were in clear disagreement with each other and becoming antagonists: over the appropriate American stance toward appeasement, over their expectations for the success of Chamberlain's policy, and over the prime minister himself. Any commitment of any kind to Britain was far from Roosevelt's mind. To encourage the democracies to stand firm against Hitler's drive, he and Hull had spoken out against aggression in their speeches of August 16 and 18 and had hoped to create uncertainty about American intentions in the case of war. But beyond this sympathetic gesture, he would not go. Although FDR wanted Britain to resist Germany, he could give it no assurance of American support if it did so. Still walking a tightrope, still watching and brooding, the president chose to remain a silent observer and to occupy himself with campaigning in Democratic primaries for supporters of the New Deal.[35]

And far from being optimistic about Chamberlain's policy, as Kennedy thought, the president was becoming increasingly pessimistic. "I'll bet three-to-one that the Germans will be able to accomplish their objectives" without a war, he predicted to Morgenthau.[36]

Roosevelt regarded Chamberlain with deep suspicion. "Chamberlain," he said, "was playing the usual game of the British—peace at any price—if he could get away with it and save his face." He "would try to place the blame on the United States for fighting or not fighting." "His inquiry to Kennedy was designed to place the blame on us, so that if they went in it was on account of the support they would have gotten from us and, if they did not, it was because we held back," FDR said, resentful of Chamberlain's repeated requests as to what his administration's attitude would be. "This is an old game," complained one State Department official, "but Joe Kennedy seems to have fallen for it."[37]

Throughout the late summer and into early fall, Roosevelt had become more and more irritated by his outspoken ambassador. "I do not think Joe is fooling him very much," wrote Ickes. FDR told him that he "did not expect Joe to last more than a couple of years in London because he was the kind of a man who liked to go from one job to another and drop it just when the going became heavy." "He also knows that Joe is enjoying his job in London, where he is having the time of his life although he cries 'wolf.'"[38] FDR's annoyance led him to regard his ambassador as an Irish-Catholic Walter Hines Page, America's classic diplomatic anglophile who looked upon the London embassy as an extension of Whitehall during World War I. The president remarked that Kennedy had been taken in by the "slippery" Chamberlain. "No matter what you say about Bingham" (Kennedy's predecessor), Roosevelt hotly insisted to Hull and Morgenthau, "he never became pro-British."[39] The president said that Kennedy was "playing the Chamberlain game" by trying to force Roosevelt's hand in Kennedy's conversations with the press. "Who would have thought that the English could take into camp a red-headed Irishman?" FDR sputtered during the Munich crisis.[40] What had begun as a friendly relationship between the two was now developing into one of barely concealed hostility. Thus, throughout the fall, the president continued his tightrope act in American foreign policy and allowed his gregarious, garrulous, and rambunctious ambassador enough slack to play out his role with little more than verbal handslapping, spanks, and rebuffs.

On the evening of September 12 Europe listened to the radio, waiting for a broadcast from Nuremberg—a broadcast in which Hitler was expected to reveal his plans for Czechoslovakia. The German chancellor made his often repeated demand that the "oppression" of the Sudeten Germans must end and that the 3.5 million "brothers" living under Czech rule must have "self-determination."[41]

The next day "spontaneous" riots erupted in Czechoslovakia and President Benes responded by establishing martial law in some of the Czech districts. British officials were alarmed and believed that German troops were ready to pounce. "The Big Four," Chamberlain, Halifax, Simon, and Hoare met in almost constant session, Kennedy reported.[42]

On the morning of September 14, Chamberlain, taking pains to keep Kennedy well informed, interrupted a cabinet meeting to tell him of a daring and unconventional plan he had decided upon. He told the ambassador that he had sent word to Hitler that he was inviting himself to Berlin to see him. The prime minister's strategy was to suggest to Hitler that the Sudetenland be given local autonomy for five years and that the German army be demobilized immediately. After five years, a final settlement should be determined by an international body. The prime minister's major concern was a "settlement for world policy": Czechoslovakia, after all, was but "a small incident in that big cause." If his "bribe" for a conference was turned down, then Britain would promise to fight alongside France, Kennedy reported.[43]

Right before the prime minister left for Berchtesgaden on September 15, Kennedy at the prompting of the British Foreign Office passed on its request for any statement that Roosevelt might make on the impending conference.[44] American officials declined to express any support for the prime minister's trip. Chamberlain was for peace at any price, Roosevelt told his cabinet, and France would join England in abandoning Czechoslovakia to Hitler's aggression. This would ensure the destruction of that country. After this international outrage, they would "wash the blood from their Judas Iscariot hands," the wily president said.[45] At the press conference that day, Hull merely said, "The historic conference today between the Prime Minister of Great Britain and the Chancellor of Germany is naturally being observed with the greatest interest by all nations which are deeply concerned in the preservation of peace."[46]

The prime minister returned from Berchtesgaden to report to the cabinet and to get its consent to Hitler's demand for self-determination for the Sudeten Germans. Although Kennedy learned that there were many rumblings and grumblings within the cabinet, it did finally accept the chancellor's demand.[47] Again in a late evening conversation with Kennedy on September 17, the prime minister asked him whether "the United States would join in" with all the other countries to protect peace and order, a request for later consideration, Kennedy told Washington.[48] "My own impression," Kennedy cabled Hull after having come from a meeting with the prime minister, "is that unless there is a terrific rise of public opinion all over the world, England does not propose to fight on the Czech issue."[49]

With consent wrung from the Czechs and after consultation with the French, Chamberlain flew to Godesberg on September 22 to continue his discussion with Hitler. Despising the prime minister as an "impertinent busybody who spoke the ridiculous jargon of an outmoded democracy,"[50] the Führer contemptuously rejected the Sudeten districts and instead presented Chamberlain with an ultimatum—the occupation of German-speaking areas by German troops by October 1. Chamberlain returned to London heavy-hearted. Initially he wanted to stand firm, but gradually he became convinced that there was no alternative but to accept—or rather to persuade the Czechs to accept. "The suspense is very marked," Kennedy cabled Hull.[51]

Roosevelt, meanwhile, decided upon a gesture. On September

26 he sent a message to Hitler, Benes, Chamberlain, and French Premier Edward Daladier: "On behalf of the one hundred thirty millions of people of the United States of America," the president said, "and for the sake of humanity everywhere, I most earnestly appeal to you not to break off negotiations. . . . So long as negotiations continue, differences may be reconciled. Once they are broken off, reason is banished and force asserts itself."[52] The next day Roosevelt sent an additional appeal personally asking the heads of state to support a conference. His request was widely accepted. Despite Hitler's vindictive diatribe to the president's September 26 message, Roosevelt sent him another message addressed only to him. FDR proposed that a conference be held in some neutral spot for all those parties directly involved in the Czech controversy and stated that "continued negotiations remain the only way by which the immediate problem can be disposed of upon any lasting basis."[53] To ward off isolationist criticism, however, Roosevelt repeated his traditional unwillingness to become involved or to assume any responsibility.

On September 27, Chamberlain too sent a reassuring message to Hitler and informed Kennedy that he had offered his services as a mediator. "You can get all essentials without war and without delay." "I am ready to come to Berlin myself at once," he plaintively wrote.[54]

As Kennedy was sitting in the packed House of Commons that afternoon to hear Chamberlain's speech, the prime minister received a message from the chancellor. Chamberlain announced to the hushed chamber that Hitler had agreed to postpone his mobilization for twenty-four hours and to meet Mussolini, French Prime Minister Daladier, and himself at a conference at Munich the next day. "I need not say what my answer will be," Chamberlain replied. Pandemonium erupted. Practically the whole house rose to give Chamberlain a standing ovation. Kennedy beamed.[55] "Everybody feels tremendously relieved tonight," Kennedy cabled Hull.[56] After his speech, Chamberlain met with his staunch supporter to thank him for his support. The prime minister insisted that "I must stay on the job for I would do much good for world peace," Kennedy wrote in his autobiography.[57] As Chamberlain prepared to leave for Germany, Roosevelt sent a congratulatory message—a terse, "Good man!"[58]

FDR, his advisers, the American public, and, of course, Kennedy, believed he deserved credit for Hitler's last-minute decision to call the Munich conference. "The President can feel that God was on his side and he was on God's side," Kennedy jubilantly wrote.[59] Roosevelt's message appealing for a conference was "the finest the President had written for a long long time." Actually, FDR's appeals were of little importance.[60] Pressure from Mussolini, along with evidence that Britain and France would eventually give in to his final demands anyhow, played the major roles in convincing the Führer to resort to negotiations rather than force. He no doubt considered Roosevelt's appeals insignificant.[61]

The "only discordant note," according to Kennedy, was from the Czech ambassador in London, Jan Masarky, who rode back from Parliament with him. He said, "I hope this doesn't mean they are going to cut us up and sell us out."[62]

As Chamberlain left for Munich, Kennedy told Halifax that he was quite hopeful about the outcome of the conference and "entirely in sympathy with, and a warm admirer of, everything the Prime Minister had done." The European situation required "a spirit of realism," he remarked, which meant doing anything necessary to preserve peace.[63]

About two o'clock in the morning of September 30 the Munich Pact was finally signed and the Czech leaders were presented with its terms. The Sudetenland was to be ceded to Germany and the Republic lost its border fortresses and was thus left defenseless.

At the prime minister's prompting, he and Hitler signed an additional agreement stating that the Munich Pact and the Anglo-German Naval Agreement were "symbolic of the desire of our two peoples never to go to war with one another again." It was to be "peace for our time."[64]

The president sent Chamberlain a congratulatory telegram. FDR instructed Kennedy to read it to Chamberlain but not to give it to him. The carefully worded statement read: "I fully share your hope and belief that here exists today the greatest opportunity in years for the establishment of a new order based on justice and on law."[65]

Although the House of Commons approved the Munich Pact by a vote of 366 to 144, profound disillusionment had set in both in and out of Parliament. Most important, however, were the changing attitudes of citizens outside Parliament. One effect of Chamberlain's proclamation of "peace for our time" was, ironically, to create a vocal demand for a speedy rearmament. "Peace for our time" became a cry that "our time" be used to rearm. Throughout that winter, air-raid shelters were improved, plans were drawn up for fire protection, for evacuation, and for the training of civilians.[66]

This gradual build-up in rearmaments lent credibility to the myth of Munich, created by Kennedy, among others, that Chamberlain's sell-out of the Czechs bought Britain precious time to rearm. Viscount Simon, one of the inner circle and the chancellor of the exchequer, offers a classic defense for the prime minister's policy. At Munich, Chamberlain "secured an invaluable twelve months in which to strengthen our preparations to wage [war]." "It was his action at Munich," Chamberlain's apologist loyally testified, "that helped to secure, more than anything else could have done, that Britain went into war against Germany as an absolutely united nation, with a united Commonwealth at her side," a position for which there is much evidence.[67] "The fact that his action did not ultimately preserve peace does not, in my judgment, affect the essential rightness of his policy at the time," wrote Simon.[68]

Throughout the rest of 1938, the disillusioned withdrew their support for appeasement—but Chamberlain's close friend and stout ally, Joe Kennedy, never withdrew his. Throughout the Czech crisis, the ambassador consistently supported Chamberlain's attempts to peacefully accommodate Hitler's demands. When asked his opinion of the Munich Pact, the ambassador later explained that Europe at that time faced either chaos or war. "And if there is any way of doing better than either of those, then it is worth trying. With me," he continued, "it is not a question of the strategy of the Munich Agreement. I am pro-peace. I pray, hope and work for peace."[69]

Kennedy's work for peace consisted of keeping Washington posted on the events in Europe, encouraging Roosevelt and Hull to support the prime minister's policy, making ostentatious calls on Halifax and Chamberlain, and conferring with other ambassadors. His efforts also included trying to frighten the Nazis by asking the president to dispatch several American cruisers to British waters and by unofficially aiding the government's censorship efforts. Yet he also undermined his efforts by telling the counselor at the German embassy in London that "his main objective was to keep America out of conflict in Europe."[70] Left to his own devices because of Roosevelt's lack of direction, Kennedy followed his own contradictory personal diplomacy.

During the Munich crisis, Roosevelt was originally a detached observer following a policy of "no risks, no commitments." As he worried and watched, hoping that the democracies would make a stand against fascism over the Sudetenland, he began to believe that war could be averted. Although he gave in to the national mood with its attention riveted on domestic problems and its preference for a passive foreign policy, he still felt compelled to make a few symbolic gestures—such as signalling that American sympathies lay with the European democracies and deploring the aggressive actions of the dictators. Although the president had hoped that the Munich Pact could create "a new order based on justice and law," he had little faith in the idea. Actually, the Sudetenland was nothing more than a way station in Germany's expansion. Hitler had already made plans to swallow the rest of Czechoslovakia. To Roosevelt, Munich was essentially a lull between storms during which the democracies must rearm.[71]

Munich was also the beginning of a new departure in American foreign policy. It encouraged FDR to reexamine the assumptions of American foreign policy and eventually to develop a policy of "methods short of war" to help Europe's democracies fight nazism. In time it led to a stiffer foreign policy for Britain as well. After Hitler defied Munich and his own declared principle of nationality by devouring the rest of Czechoslovakia in March 1939, Chamberlain reluctantly guaranteed Poland's independence. This new policy committed Britain to positive action in Eastern Europe and seemed to mean, if not the end of appeasement, then at least its abatement.

NOTES

1. The standard treatments of the 1938 Czech crisis include: John Wheeler-Bennett, *Munich: Prologue to Tragedy* (New York: Duell, Sloan & Pearce, 1948); R.G.D. Laffan, *The Crisis over Czechoslovakia, January to September, 1938* (Oxford, Eng.: Oxford University Press, 1951); Keith Eubank, *Munich* (Norman: University of Oklahoma Press, 1963); and Telford Taylor, *Munich* (New York: Doubleday, 1979). The standard reference on American appeasement is Arnold Offner, *American Appeasement: United States Foreign Policy and Germany, 1933–1938* (New York: W. W. Norton, 1969).

2. A.J.P. Taylor, *Origins of the Second World War* (New York: Atheneum, 1962).

3. William Rock, "British Appeasement (1930's); A Need for Revision?" *The South Atlantic Quarterly* 78, no. 3 (Summer 1979): 298.

4. Robert Dallek, *Franklin D. Roosevelt and American Foreign Policy, 1932–1945* (New York: Oxford University Press, 1979), p. 162.

5. Keith Middlemas, *The Strategy of Appeasement* (Chicago: Quadrangle Books, 1972), p. 285.

6. Portions of this chapter have been published in Jane Karoline Vieth, "Munich Revisited through Joseph P. Kennedy's Eyes," *Michigan Academician* 18, no. 1 (Winter 1986): 73–85; and in Vieth, "Joseph P. Kennedy and British Appeasement: The Diplomacy of a Boston Irishman," in *U.S. Diplomats in Europe, 1919–1941*, edited by Kenneth Paul Jones (Santa Barbara, Calif.: ABC-Clio, 1981), pp. 165–82. Some excellent books on the life and times of Joseph Kennedy are Michael R. Beschloss, *Kennedy and Roosevelt: The Uneasy Alliance* (New York: W. W. Norton, 1980); Doris Kearns Goodwin, *The Fitzgeralds and the Kennedys: An American Saga* (New York: Simon and Schuster, 1987); and Richard J. Whalen, *The Founding Father: The Story of Joseph P. Kennedy* (New York: The New American Library, 1964).

7. Winston S. Churchill, *The Gathering Storm* (New York: Bantam Books, 1961), pp. 251–52.

8. David Reynolds, *The Creation of the Anglo-American Alliance 1937–41* (Chapel Hill: University of North Carolina Press, 1982), p. 33.

9. Keith Feiling, *The Life of Neville Chamberlain* (London: Macmillan, 1970), p. 343.

10. Great Britain, *Parliamentary Debates* (Commons), 5th Series, March 24,

1938, vol. 33, pp. 1405–6; The Earl of Birkenhead, *Halifax* (London: Hamish Hamilton, 1965), p. 383.

11. Herschel V. Johnson to Hull, March 25, 1938, 123/59, U.S. Department of State (hereafter cited as USDS).

12. U.S. Department of State, *Foreign Relations of the United States: Diplomatic Papers, 1938* (Washington, D.C.: U.S. Government Printing Office, 1955), March 23, 1938, vol. 1, p. 40 (hereafter cited as *FRUS*).

13. *FRUS*, September 26, 1938, vol. 1, p. 661.

14. *FRUS*, May 28, 1938, vol. 1, pp. 520–21.

15. Walter Millis, *The Forrestal Diaries* (New York: Viking Press, 1951), pp. 121–22.

16. Arthur Krock, *Memoirs* (New York: Funk & Wagnalls, 1968), p. 334.

17. *The Secret Diary of Harold L. Ickes* (New York: Simon and Schuster, 1954), June 26, 1938, vol. 2, pp. 405–6.

18. *New York Post*, January 11, 1961, as cited in Whalen, p. 228.

19. I have seen no evidence of Kennedy's assessment of the meeting.

20. U.S. Government Printing Office, *Documents on German Foreign Policy, 1918–1945: From the Archives of the German Foreign Ministry*, Series D (London: H.M.S.O., 1949), June 13, 1938, vol. 1, pp. 714–18 (hereafter cited as *German Documents*); Offner, pp. 251–52; *Newsweek*, "The Mystery of Joe Kennedy," September 12, 1960, p. 29.

21. *German Documents*, pp. 721–23.

22. Ibid., p. 718.

23. Kennedy to Hull, July 26, 1938, 800 General, USDS.

24. *FRUS*, July 29, 1938, vol. 1, pp. 537–39.

25. *FRUS*, August 29, 1938, vol. 1, pp. 560–61.

26. E. L. Woodward and Rohan Butler, *Documents on British Foreign Policy*, 3rd Series (London: 1938) September 2, 1938, vol. 2, p. 213 (hereafter cited as *British Documents*); Great Britain, Public Record Office, Foreign Office Series 371: Political, American, United States; 371-228/2099 *Annual Report for 1938*, pp. 8–36.

27. *British Documents*, pp. 212–13; Middlemas, p. 285.

28. Middlemas, p. 285; *FRUS*, August 29, 1938, vol. 1, pp. 560–61.

29. Kennedy to Hull, August 31, 1938, 800 Czechoslovakia, USDS.

30. Hull to Kennedy, September 1, 1938, 123/Kennedy, Joseph P. 109, USDS.

31. Hull, pp. 587–88.

32. Hull to Kennedy, September 1, 1938, 123/Kennedy, Joseph P. 109, USDS.

33. Kennedy to Hull, September 10, 1938, 800 Czechoslovakia, USDS.

34. *Morgenthau Diary*, September 1, 1938, 138/35.

35. Dallek, pp. 162–66.

36. *Morgenthau Diary*, September 1, 1938, vol. 138, p. 34, Franklin D. Roosevelt Library (hereafter cited as FDRL).
37. J. P. Moffat, *The Moffat Papers*, ed. Nancy H. Hooker (Cambridge, Mass.: Harvard University Press, 1956), p. 203.
38. *Ickes Diary*, July 16, 1938, vol. 2, p. 415.
39. "The Morgenthau Diary," *Colliers*, vol. 138, p. 34, FDRL.
40. *Morgenthau Diary*, September 11, 1938, vol. 138, p. 34.
41. *The New York Times*, September 13, 1938, p. 1.
42. *FRUS*, September 13, 1938, vol. 1, p. 592.
43. Kennedy to Hull, September 14, 1938, 800 Czechoslovakia, USDS; Kennedy to Hull, September 14, 1938, Great Britain, FDRL.
44. Hull, p. 589.
45. *Ickes Diary*, vol. 2, pp. 467–78; Adolf Berle, *Navigating the Rapids, 1981–1971* (New York: Harcourt Brace Jovanovich, 1973), p. 184.
46. Hull, p. 589; *FRUS*, September 15, 1938, vol. 1, p. 605.
47. Kennedy to Hull, September 17, 1938, 1:00 P.M., 800 Czechoslovakia, USDS; Kennedy to Hull, September 17, 1938, FDRL.
48. Kennedy to Hull, September 17, 1938, 10:00 P.M., 800 Czechoslovakia, USDS.
49. Kennedy to Hull, September 17, 1938, PSF, Box 10, FDRL; Kennedy to Hull, September 19, 1938, vol. 1, p. 622.
50. F. S. Northedge, *The Troubled Giant* (London: G. Bell & Sons, 1966), p. 531.
51. Kennedy to Hull, September 23, 1938, 800 Czechoslovakia, USDS.
52. Hull, p. 592.
53. Ibid., p. 593.
54. Feiling, p. 372; *FRUS*, September 28, 1938, vol. 1, p. 688.
55. Joseph P. Kennedy, *The Landis Papers*, chap. 17, n.p., Manuscript Division, Library of Congress; Whalen, p. 237.
56. Kennedy to Hull, September 28, 1938, 800 Czechoslovakia, 69–92, USDS.
57. *The Landis Papers*, chap. 17.
58. *FRUS*, September 28, 1938, vol. 1, p. 688.
59. Ibid., p. 693; Kennedy to Hull, September 28, 1938, 800 Czechoslovakia, 58, USDS; Hull, p. 595; *Ickes Diary*, September 30, 1938, vol. 2, p. 479; Dallek, p. 166.
60. Dallek, p. 166.
61. Kennedy to Hull, September 28, 1938, 800 Czechoslovakia, USDS; *FRUS*, September 28, 1938, vol. 1, p. 693.
62. *British Documents*, Series 3, vol. 11, pp. 524–35.
63. Feiling, p. 381.
64. Vieth, "Munich Revisited through Joseph P. Kennedy's Eyes," p. 83.

65. Churchill, pp. 292, 294–95.

66. Ritchie Ovendale, *"Appeasement" and the English Speaking World* (Cardiff: University of Wales Press, 1975); Vieth, "Joseph P. Kennedy and British Appeasement," pp. 165–66, 180–82; Rock, "British Appeasement (1930's); A Need for Revision?", pp. 290–301.

67. Viscount Simon, *Retrospect: The Memoirs of the Rt. Hon. Viscount Simon* (London: Hutchinson, 1952), pp. 238–39.

68. *The New York Times*, December 16, 1938, p. 13.

69. *German Documents*, Series D, vol. 1, p. 713.

70. Dallek, p. 171.

71. Ibid.

4

"Speaking the Same Language": The U.S. Response to the Italo-Ethiopian War and the Origins of American Appeasement

David F. Schmitz

The fiftieth anniversary of the outbreak of World War II provides an excellent vantage point from which to reexamine different aspects of United States foreign policy and the coming of the war. With the exception of the negative response to the Italo-Ethiopian war, the Roosevelt administration's policy toward Fascist Italy has been a generally overlooked aspect of the American response to the worldwide crisis of the 1930s. By focusing narrowly on Italy's aggression in Africa, scholars have misinterpreted United States policy toward Italy during the 1930s and, consequently, dismissed its significance to Roosevelt's overall European policy. As the following analysis will demonstrate, however, it is incorrect to conclude that the United States adopted an anti-Italian policy in the wake of the Italo-Ethiopian war and that Italy was unimportant to America's appeasement policy toward Germany.

The Italo-Ethiopian war forced Franklin D. Roosevelt and his foreign policy advisors to focus more attention on Europe and the danger of a general European conflict. The Italian invasion of Ethiopia was viewed by American policymakers as an imperialist war. It was also seen as a mistaken policy by Italy, not just naked aggression, for American officials did not believe that it served Italy's real interests or represented the true nature of Mussolini's regime. The concern in Washington was to prevent the tensions caused by the Abyssinian war to broaden into a conflict between Italy and Britain. American policy, therefore, was to morally condemn the Italian war while avoiding any actions which would force further Italian aggression or cause a permanent break in relations. This brush with another European war in twenty years marked the beginning of the United States's effort at economic appeasement in Europe as a means to help settle the crisis of German resurgence.[1] Italy played a significant role in that policy.

The decision to adopt a policy of appeasement was based upon the American understanding of fascism gained from relations with Italy since 1922, and the Roosevelt administration's fear that another world war would lead to a protracted postwar era of social unrest and revolution. The prior American analysis of fascism as a stabilizing force in Italy which had prevented a Bolshevik triumph in Rome, and fear of a general European war, led to efforts to improve relations with Italy after the Italian conquest of Ethiopia. The administration believed that Mussolini was a "moderate" Fascist who did not desire war, and who could influence Hitler to soften German demands and find a peaceful solution to their grievances.[2] A reexamination of United States relations with Fascist Italy after 1935, therefore, is key to understanding both what American leaders thought about fascism, and why they believed appeasement could work and insure American interests in Europe.

Studies concerned with the American response to Italy's aggression on the horn of Africa have concentrated on the question of whether or not American policy played a role in the failure of the League of Nations to restrain Mussolini.[3] The related question of the impact of the Italo-Ethiopian war on Congressional neutrality legislation has also drawn much attention.[4] Given this, the Italian invasion of Ethiopia in October 1935, has been seen as marking the end of friendly U.S.–Italian relations and the beginning of an anti-Fascist policy by the Roosevelt administration. President Roosevelt and Secretary of State Cordell Hull both opposed the Italian action and placed the full blame for the hostilities on Italy. In addition, they openly sympathized with the plight of Ethiopia, and sought to hamper the Italian war effort by invoking the Neutrality Act of

1935 to embargo military supplies and by calling for a moral boycott in trade of war-related materials. By studying American policy only during the immediate crisis these works fail to recognize that the strained relations were temporary. They did not cause American policymakers to reevaluate their favorable assumptions and views on Mussolini and fascism in Italy. Italian-American relations, therefore, were not permanently damaged by the war. Indeed, the Roosevelt administration actively sought to restore friendly relations with Italy as part of its overall peace efforts in Europe.

The first two studies of American policy toward the Italo-Ethiopian crisis, Henderson B. Braddick, "A New Look at American Policy During the Italo-Ethiopian Crisis, 1935–1936" and Robert A. Friedlander, "New Light on the Anglo-American Reaction to the Ethiopian War, 1935–1936," reflect the debates of the 1930s and the views of the internationalists who sought a more active American role in world events. Both center their investigations on how American policy influenced British policy and the actions taken by the League of Nations. Each author found that while American policy was cautious and at times contradictory, the United States opposed Mussolini's action because Britain required support against Italy.[5] American officials believed that by supporting Britain, London would be more inclined to support American policy in the Pacific, and that "Mussolini would almost inevitably succumb to British pressure."[6] Roosevelt and Hull sought to preserve U.S. independence from the League of Nations to avoid domestic public criticism while also supporting any sanctions taken against Italy. The authors agree with the interpretations of internationalists or orthodox historians that posit that Roosevelt opposed Italian and German actions but was restricted by public opinion from taking a more active role. It was not, therefore, due to America's unwillingness to join directly with the League of Nations that caused collective security to fail.

Although neither article addresses the larger question of U.S.–Italian relations, implicit in their arguments is that the war led to a change or even a reversal of American policy. Braddick notes that prior to 1935 relations between Mussolini and Roosevelt "had been very friendly" but that because of the Ethiopian crisis the "administration had taken sides against Fascist Italy."[7] American policy, therefore, while not openly aligned with collective security, had taken the first steps toward an anti-Fascist position or coalition.

Braddick and Friedlander's arguments are supported by Brice Harris's *The United States and the Italo-Ethiopian Crisis*. Harris's work is the most comprehensive study of American policy toward the Abyssinian war. His main concern was with what part the United States played in the development of British policy and whether "the lack of positive and forthright" American cooperation with the League of Nations was responsible for the organization's failure to restrain Mussolini.[8] Harris concluded that American officials, while often cautious prisoners of an isolationist public, sought to encourage a firm British position. Washington mainly followed London's policy and was not responsible for the collapse of the League of Nations's sanctions and its failure to halt Italian aggression. Still, he found that the American response was limited and that the Roosevelt administration was unwilling to take the one step, an oil embargo, that could have seriously hampered Italy's war effort.

Why the administration was not ready to cut off oil and join the League of Nations in an oil embargo is the key to the problem. Harris contended that a combination of domestic pressures to stay clear of the League of Nations, the desire to maintain an independent policy, and fear that an oil cutoff would lead to a war between Italy and Britain prevented Roosevelt and Hull from taking such a step. Preventing a war in the Mediterranean was the most important, because Harris had already demonstrated that the administration could support the League's actions without direct cooperation. Yet this point remained unexplored and the events are not discussed in the larger framework of Roosevelt's policy toward Italy.

Harris noted that until 1935 U.S.–Italian relations were "on excellent terms," but that "the Fascist program of aggressive expansion in 1935 signaled the turning point in Italian-American relations."[9] However, he did not investigate the larger context of

American policy toward Italy. He relied upon the unpublished dissertation of Louis A. De Santi, "United States Relations with Italy under Mussolini, 1922–1941," in reaching his conclusion. De Santi, using only certain State Department records available immediately after the war, concluded that after 1935 the United States refused "to be friends with the enemy of [its] friends and allies . . . . in fact workable relations between the two countries proved impossible."[10] Thus, the tensions and opposition to Italy's colonial conquest became the basis for and the beginning of an anti-Italian policy.

De Santi's interpretation was also adopted by John Diggins in his path-breaking study of American popular opinion on Mussolini, *Mussolini and Fascism: The View from America.* Diggins found that America's favorable opinion of Mussolini declined quickly after 1935, paralleling the more skeptical views of policymakers and the deterioration of relations between Washington and Rome.[11] This interpretation found its most ardent advocate in Rolfe Buzzell's unpublished dissertation, "The Eagle and the Fasces: The United States and Italy, 1935–1939." Buzzell argued that after the Ethiopia war, relations changed

from outward cordiality to open distrust and smoldering antagonism. Italy's invasion of Ethiopia in 1935 brought to the surface the underlying differences with the United States and altered formerly friendly American attitudes toward Benito Mussolini . . . and his Fascist regime.

The Roosevelt administration, Buzzell continued, took a hard line with Italy after 1935 that blocked any chance of successfully splitting the Axis. "Failing to exploit Italy's position as the weak link in the Axis relations, officials in Washington made no sustained effort to encourage or reward an Italian foreign policy independent of Germany."[12]

This interpretation has become the standard understanding of United States policy toward Fascist Italy during the 1930s. It has both drawn on the views of traditional understandings of United

States policy, such as William L. Langer and S. Everett Gleason's
The Challenge to Isolation,[13] and reinforced those views in more
recent studies, as in Robert Dallek's *Franklin D.
Roosevelt and American Foreign Policy, 1932–1945*.[14] Even studies that reject
the traditional viewpoint and see American policy as appeasement
generally overlook the role of Italy. All of the studies of United
States appeasement of Germany pass over the American experience with Fascist Italy prior to the invasion of Ethiopia and its
influence on American officials' views concerning Hitler and
Nazism, and why policymakers, therefore, believed there was a
possibility of a successful accommodation with Germany. Moreover, they overlook the role Italy played in the actual American
appeasement policy during the 1930s.[15]

All the studies reviewed agree that American policy was not
consistent in its response to the crisis in Ethiopia and that American
leaders failed to do all they could to hamper Italy's war effort and,
in fact, did nothing to aid Ethiopia. But these studies fail to explain
why this happened and, therefore, incorrectly conclude that U.S.–
Italian relations were damaged. The reason for ambiguity in American policy rested in the fact that American policymakers sought
to restrain Italy *without* damaging relations. In other words, they
sought to demonstrate to Mussolini their displeasure while also
continuing to insist that Italy's best means to accomplishing its
goals was through cooperation with the Western democracies. This
would allow American officials to focus on the greater problems
of European recovery and Germany. The policy itself was inter-
nally contradictory, but the desire for continued good relations
with Italy was much more important than Ethiopia's independence.

When the Italo-Ethiopian war is examined in the context of
relations with Italy prior to the war, and the general desires of the
Roosevelt administration to develop an appeasement policy to
secure long-term peace in Europe, American policy becomes
understandable. Prior good relations, the belief that Mussolini was
a moderate who desired peace, and the conviction that the Italian
dictator held a constructive influence over his German counterpart
placed Italy in a key position in American policymakers' plans for

a European settlement. The Italo-Ethiopian war caused difficulties for American officials, but it did not modify these beliefs. The Roosevelt administration inherited excellent relations with Mussolini from the Republicans. Former Secretary of State Henry L. Stimson recalled that "the Italians in 1931 and 1932 were of all the great continental powers the least difficult," and that Mussolini was "a sound and useful leader."[16] The Fascists' rise to power in 1922 was welcomed by most United States officials. Mussolini and his followers were viewed as nationalists who would provide for the maintenance of social order, a bulwark against bolshevism, and an antidote for the illness of weak government in Italy. The State Department analyzed the Fascist party as being divided into two groups, "moderates" and "extremists." The "extremists" were blamed for the more unsavory aspects of Italian fascism. The "moderates," led by Mussolini, could be counted upon to keep Italy's policies on a safe course which featured domestic stability, antibolshevism, and cooperation with the United States.

This analysis allowed American officials to ignore the fact that Mussolini's government brutally repressed all opposition groups, destroyed Italy's constitutional government, and ruled by means of violence. In developing American policy, officials in Washington were mainly influenced by Mussolini's establishment of a stable, non-Communist government that welcomed American trade and investments. In addition, the State Department believed that Mussolini's chest-beating speeches on foreign policy were made only for Italian domestic consumption and to appease the more extreme elements of the party. The Roosevelt administration further believed that Mussolini would provide a moderating influence on Hitler.[17]

In June 1933, in a letter to Ambassador to Italy Breckinridge Long, Roosevelt outlined his opinion of Mussolini. The president saw the Italian dictator as a moderate nationalist whose rule was having a positive impact on Italy. In addition, Roosevelt saw Mussolini as a leader who would strive to maintain peace in Europe. The president wrote that he was "deeply impressed by what [Mussolini] has accomplished and by his evidenced honest purpose of restoring Italy and seeking to prevent general European trouble."[18] In September, Roosevelt wrote Long that with regard to disarmament and an overall European peace, "I feel that [Mussolini] can accomplish more than anyone else."[19]

Italy's mobilization of its army on the Brenner Pass frontier with Austria in July 1934 cemented the view of Mussolini as a peacemaker who held a constructive influence over Hitler. Mussolini's action was seen as the decisive step which caused Hitler to abort his attempt to absorb Austria into the German Reich. Under Secretary of State William Phillips noted the prevailing opinion of policymakers that it was Mussolini's action "which made Hitler realize that he could not fool with the Austrian State."[20] Necessary revisions of the Versailles treaty would have to be accomplished by peaceful means. A February 1935 State Department report summarized these views when it noted that fascism in Italy was necessary due to the fact that parliamentary government "was unsuited to Italian political life," the danger of bolshevism, and the need for stability. Moreover, Italy now held the "key position in the European concert" due to its relations with Germany and the problems of Central Europe. "Italy not infrequently holds and aims to keep the balance of power in Europe."[21]

The approach of the Italo-Ethiopian war forced President Roosevelt to give more attention to the building international crisis in Europe and Italy's position. In March 1935, he wrote Breckinridge Long that

> these are without doubt the most hair trigger times the world has gone through in your life time or mine. I do not even exclude June and July, 1914, because at that time there was economic and social stability, with only the loom of war by Governments in accordance with preconceived ideas and prognostications. Today there is not one element alone but three or more.[22]

Long replied that he agreed with this point and that he too was worried that with "social unrest as widespread as it is, and with the certain exaggeration of it as the sequel to another war," he could "only shudder to think of our social situation a year after another conflict."[23]

Roosevelt did not fully elaborate on what the three or more elements were in his letter to Long. An examination of his writings on the question in 1935 and 1936, however, yields a general picture of the president worried that with the lack of economic and social stability in Europe due to the Great Depression, the aftermath of another world war would prove to be even more revolutionary than the post-World War I era. On October 2, 1935, Roosevelt spoke in San Diego, California, about the danger of a "fierce foreign war" that was a "present danger at this moment to the future of civilization." Reflecting his concern about the crisis in Africa, Roosevelt referred to the Great War as "the folly of twenty years ago," and argued that the current danger in Europe was even greater than the outbreak and disruption of that war. A repeat would "drag civilization to a level from which world wide recovery may be all but impossible."[24]

The outbreak of fighting in Africa prompted the President to make a major foreign policy speech on Armistice Day, 1935. Roosevelt emphasized that people must come to understand "that the elation and prosperity which may come from a new war must lead—for those who survive it—to economic and social collapse more sweeping than anywhere experienced in the past."[25] The following February Roosevelt wrote Ambassador to France Jesse Straus concerning his fears for Europe. "One cannot help feeling that the whole European panorama is fundamentally blacker than any time in your life time or mine." He then compared the current crisis first with the revolutions of 1848 and then the Great War. "In 1848 revolutions in a dozen countries synchronized because of a general European demand for constitutional representative government; but at that time economics, budgets, foreign exchange and industrialism were not in the picture and the problem was ten times more simple than it is today. In 1914 the situation was eighty percent military, and again vastly simpler than today." His conclusion was that these "may be the last days of the period of peace before a long chaos."[26] The president feared another war because of the chaos it would bring to Europe. These communications marked the beginning of a search for a peace policy.

Cordell Hull shared the president's pessimism, and a similar view shaped the State Department's reaction to the approaching Italo-Ethiopian war. Hull recalled in his memoirs that his greatest worry during 1935, while the crisis on the horn of Africa mounted, was that it might somehow expand into a conflict between Italy and Great Britain. As Hull explained the American attitude to the French ambassador in July 1935, "A war between Italy and Ethiopia would be bad enough, but it is entirely within the range of possibility that it would in due time spread back into more than one part of Europe with its unimaginable, devastating effects."[27] It was not the Italian domination of Ethiopia which primarily concerned Hull, but the danger of the military conflict spreading.

Mussolini's plans for the conquest of Ethiopia were well known to American officials by the time of the December 1934 border clash at Wal-Wal between Italian and Ethiopian forces which marked the beginning of the crisis. This allowed President Roosevelt and the State Department ample time to decide upon a policy toward Italy's aggression on the horn of Africa. The major concern and the center of all discussions was how Mussolini's actions would influence events in Europe. Ethiopia itself, as will be demonstrated, was of little concern to American officials.

Ambassador Long kept both President Roosevelt and Secretary of State Hull fully informed of Italian plans and the reactions of various European nations. Long's correspondence concentrated on why the United States should not oppose Italy's colonial expansion. Italy's taking of African colonies, Long noted, was no different from British or French actions at an earlier time. Moreover, the important concerns of the United States were in Europe and the problem of Germany. Mussolini's actions in Africa should be tolerated because he held influence over Hitler and should not be alienated over a matter of no immediate interest to the United States. Too harsh a policy would push Mussolini toward Hitler and an alliance of the dictators.[28]

Long consistently focused the discussion onto Germany, the key to the building European crisis. He argued that France and its allies "have put a military ring around Germany" and that without concessions "war is the only cure for the malady with which Europe is affected."[29] Germany would have to be appeased and Italy's role would be key. It was unwise, therefore, to oppose Mussolini and push him into a position through sanctions that might lead to a failure of his policy. This could force him to lash out in frustration against Britain and bring about a larger war. Besides, Long noted, it was clear that the French had given Mussolini a free hand in Ethiopia.[30]

The State Department agreed with the ambassador's analysis and adopted a conciliatory position toward Italy leading up to the war. Prior to the actual fighting, State Department officials downplayed the importance of the coming war and sought to avoid any identification of the United States with Ethiopia. The leaders of the Department's Western European Division, J. Pierrepont Moffat and James Clement Dunn, opposed any actions against Italy, both out of sympathy for Italy's needs and fear of the fighting spreading to Europe. Moffat argued in March that he did not believe "that Italy intended to start a war of conquest" beyond Ethiopia because that conflict would take up all of Italy's resources.[31]

Moffat also believed that while an Italian victory in Ethiopia would be bad for peace, in that it might encourage aggression, an Italian defeat might be worse. Defeat "would undoubtedly bring in its train not only revolution to Italy, but it would also bring nearer the inevitable day of German aggression." In addition, as Moffat wrote William Castle, an Italian defeat would be a disaster for European peace because "a strong Italy would seem to be essential in the eventual solution of the far more serious German problem."[32] Under Secretary of State Phillips summed up the State Department's view of the Italo-Ethiopian war when he noted that the Department saw "Mussolini's 'enterprise' as a detail and felt that Germany remained the key to the whole European situation."[33] Italy's influence could not be squandered over Ethiopia.

Ethiopian ruler Haile Selassie tried twice during the summer of

1935 to entangle the United States on Ethiopia's side. Desperately seeking support beyond the apparently meaningless League of Nations' efforts at arbitration, Selassie's first attempt was a call upon the United States in July 1935 to invoke the Kellogg-Briand Pact of 1928, a multinational agreement renouncing war. Grasping for straws, Selassie hoped that because the United States had been the original sponsor of the pact it would not turn its back on its provisions. This would force the United States to take sides against Italy and hopefully push the League of Nations to some effective collective action prior to the actual outbreak of fighting.

Secretary of State Hull responded that the United States still believed that the Kellogg-Briand Pact was binding. But the secretary turned down the offer to take any action upon it. As he informed the British, "the United States Government had no disposition to get in the way of the British Government" while it sought to "compose this controversy." Hull's official response noted that the United States was "gratified that the League of Nations . . . has given its attention to the controversy," and that the League of Nations would no doubt reach a decision that would allow a settlement in the spirit of the Kellogg-Briand Pact.[34]

The American embassy in Rome notified Hull that the Italian government took his message to mean that the United States would not interfere in any way in the matter. Italy believed that the "American Government realizes the futility of any effort to arrest Mussolini's resolute and upright action." While Hull responded that "no one speaking for the State Department has made any statement" such as the position reported, he did not reject this as an accurate interpretation of American hopes that the crisis would be resolved without American involvement.[35]

Selassie again attempted to involve the United States when in late August Ethiopia granted Standard Vacuum Oil Company of New Jersey a seventy-five year mineral exploitation concession. The State Department reacted immediately to isolate the United States government from any connection with the deal. Standard Oil, failing to obtain any assurances of its rights from the Roosevelt administration, agreed with the State Department on September 3 to withdraw from the agreement. On September 5, Hull sought to make the American position clear to Ethiopia. He instructed the American chargé d'affaires in Ethiopia, C. Van H. Engert, to inform Selassie that American policy was meant to be "helpful to the cause of peace," and not "helpful to Ethiopia" as Engert had previously informed him.[36]

In August, Roosevelt did attempt to intervene to prevent war in Africa through a direct appeal to Mussolini. He asked Mussolini to find a means short of war for obtaining Italy's objectives. It was not Italy's ambitions that were called into question, but the methods and the fact that Mussolini might not be able to keep the conflict from engulfing the whole Mediterranean. The Italian dictator rejected Roosevelt's plea, arguing that Italy's prestige was at stake and that it was, therefore, too late for him to call off his military plans. If he demobilized, other nations would no longer take Italy seriously.[37]

On October 3, 1935, Italy invaded Ethiopia. Roosevelt's hopes that Mussolini would respond to reasoned arguments that Italy's actions were based upon miscalculations of its best interests were broken for the time. News of the attack reached the president while he was vacationing on board the *USS Houston*, and he reacted angrily. He immediately instructed Hull to invoke the recently passed Neutrality Act in order to deny Italy access to American arms.[38] He did not wait for an official declaration of war, telling Harry Hopkins, "They are dropping bombs on Ethiopia—and that is war. Why wait for Mussolini to say so?"[39] In addition, Roosevelt issued a warning to American citizens against travel on belligerent ships and told American traders that they conducted business with the belligerents at their own risk. Inasmuch as Ethiopia had no passenger shipping or access to American trade, both measures were directed against Italy. In October and November, Secretary Hull called for a "moral embargo" on the shipment of war-related items, including oil, copper, and scrap steel.

The administration would not, however, take any further steps, such as imposing an oil embargo that would cripple Italy's war machine. Actions were limited so as to not antagonize Mussolini to the point that he would precipitate a war with Britain or break relations. As Ambassador Long noted, an oil embargo would force Italy "to an early action and bring on a European war." Thus, in November, when Britain asked the United States if it would join an oil sanction, Hull informed the Foreign Office that the United States would not participate in or support any such action by league members. While cooperating independently on other matters, the United States was not willing to take this crucial step.[40] Shortly after Hull's rebuke came the disastrous Hoare-Laval peace plan. It was a secret plan devised by the British and French to partition Ethiopia and grant Italy economic dominance there. Only a strong negative reaction by the British public when word leaked out prevented the deal from being completed.[41]

Roosevelt and Hull felt betrayed by Mussolini's aggression. But it was Mussolini's methods and not his objective which led to Roosevelt's anger and the decision to try and isolate Italy. The greater concern in Washington was European affairs. Along with their worry that Italy's actions might lead to a larger war, State Department officials were concerned that active opposition to Mussolini might lead to domestic unrest in Italy that could only benefit the left. American leaders saw the whole adventure as a colonial war and a misguided policy. Hull's meeting on November 22, 1935, with the Italian ambassador provided a clear demonstration of the administration's anger, understanding of the war, and its unwillingness to revise its analysis of Mussolini and fascism.

Hull was astonished that the Italian ambassador had come to the State Department to protest that the application of the Neutrality Laws discriminated against Italy. The secretary noted that both he and Roosevelt had pleaded with Mussolini to avoid war and obtain Italy's objectives through other means but had been ignored. Now Mussolini "expects us to furnish him with war supplies." Hull recalled his peace efforts, stating that

   during the last three years I had almost worn myself out
   physically in an effort to aid in world economic rehabilitation
   so that Italy and other countries would have an adequate

amount of international trade to afford contentment to their respective populations . . . The Ambassador could not begin to imagine the deep disappointment I feel at the effort to renew the practice which all nations have recently undertaken to abandon, related to that of military aggression by any and all countries at any and all times.

Hull noted that he could not understand why Italy did not use economic means to accomplish its objectives of domination in Ethiopia, "why [the Italian] Government had not taken $100,000,000 to Ethiopia and brought back a key to the entire Empire instead of expending several hundred million dollars in its military conquest with all the worry and threat of danger to the balance of the world."[42]

Because Mussolini's Ethiopian adventure was viewed as a misguided policy and America's overriding concern was with European affairs, it was not surprising that Roosevelt and Hull soon swallowed their anger. There was, therefore, no reevaluation of the favorable analysis of Mussolini as a "moderate" Fascist sincere in his desire for peace. Long-range European goals guided American efforts to improve the strained relations with Italy, and by 1937 the old analysis of Mussolini as a moderate was again directing American policy toward Italy. Moreover, the improvement of relations with Italy was seen as necessary in order to use Mussolini as a moderating influence on Hitler. Not even aid to Franco's Fascist rebels in Spain would shake that view.

The key officials in the effort to restore good relations were the former under secretary of state and new ambassador to Italy, William Phillips, and the new Under Secretary of State Sumner Welles. Both men were close personal friends of the president, and leading State Department advocates of appeasement and the continued isolation of the Soviet Union from European affairs. Phillips's appointment was a signal to Rome that while the United States opposed Italy's aggression in Africa and would not recognize Italian control, European affairs were of much greater importance, and that Washington sought to continue good relations with Italy.

Phillips wrote a series of favorable reports and letters to Roosevelt and the State Department concerning Mussolini and fascism, demonstrating that Mussolini's image as a peacemaker and a moderate remained intact. In January 1937, Phillips wrote Roosevelt that while fascism as a "form of government is anything but desirable from our point of view, I am greatly impressed by the efforts of Mussolini to improve the conditions of the masses." Phillips concluded that the Fascists "honestly believe that they represent a true democracy in as much as the welfare of the people is their principal objective. Certainly they have much evidence in their favor."[43]

Turning to foreign policy, Phillips wrote in April that while Mussolini continued to use strident language when making public speeches, his "bellicose language and the rattling of the sword . . . is in [Mussolini's] opinion necessary to keep alive [the] new spirit of the Italian people," which had emerged under fascism.[44] Ambassador Phillips was reviving the old pre-Ethiopia argument that Mussolini's words were merely for domestic consumption, and that they had little correlation to how he would act. That is, while Mussolini may engage in small colonial wars to rally the Italian people to the Fascist state, Phillips believed that he had no intention of bringing Italy into a war with any European nation.

The ambassador had little but praise for Mussolini and his programs. He believed that Fascism had brought the Italian people out of a "slough of despond," and had created a new, proud spirit in Italy. "Through his dynamic personality and great human qualities," Phillips wrote Roosevelt, Mussolini "has created a new and vigorous race throughout Italy. He is essentially interested in bettering conditions of the masses and his accomplishments in this direction are astounding and are a source of constant amazement to me." Phillips concluded that Mussolini had no further aggressive intentions. Fascist aid to Francisco Franco's rebellion in Spain was not to be understood as part of a policy of aggression. Mussolini's only intention in Spain, the ambassador argued, was to prevent the establishment of a Communist state in the Mediterranean. Phillips concluded that Mussolini, desiring to concentrate on domestic matters, was already tired of the war in Spain.[45]

The State Department concurred with the new ambassador's analysis. Hugh R. Wilson openly admired Italy's achievements in Ethiopia, writing that "the Italian effort was magnificent, the road construction was superlative, the health of the Army something that had never been seen when Westerners were fighting in tropic conditions."[46] James Dunn noted that Mussolini's intention to remove his forces from Spain indicated that he was "sincerely on the side of peace."[47] In a June 1937 report, the State Department reiterated the analysis of fascism which had guided its policy since 1922. Fascism "has brought order out of chaos, discipline out of license, and solvency out of bankruptcy." In foreign affairs, "Italy is serving her own interests and not those of Germany." Italy's importance in influencing Germany and in maintaining the peace of Europe should not, therefore, be undercut by an unfriendly policy.[48]

Phillips sought to improve relations based upon this understanding of Italy's action. He recommended that the trade treaty negotiations between the United States and Italy which were suspended due to the outbreak of war in Africa be reopened. The State Department agreed and talks with Rome resumed during the summer of 1937. In May, Phillips wrote the State Department that "it is exceedingly important at the present moment that there be a sympathetic ear at the Department to the changed attitude" in Italy toward trade.[49] Hull responded that he was "taking a personal interest in these negotiations," and that he would "see that our work goes along as fast as possible."[50] A treaty was completed that summer but the United States refused to finalize it. Assistant Secretary of State Francis Sayre, who was in charge of the negotiations, wrote Phillips that "as you know the whole international situation has been of grave concern to the Secretary" and that "he feels it would be unwise to bind our hands by entering into a treaty with Italy at least for the present."[51] Hull did not share Sayre's views, though, and approved the signing of the treaty with Italy in November.[52] The treaty was never completed, however, due to the

Roosevelt administration's refusal to grant recognition of the king of Italy as also the emperor of Ethiopia. The United States decision not to finalize the agreement had little to do with a concern of binding American hands to Italy, or an anti-Italian attitude. During the summer of 1937, President Roosevelt began to listen more to the advice of Sumner Welles on international affairs. It was Welles's belief that Mussolini and Italy were the key to a general European peace settlement. The under secretary hoped that Italy could be used as the swing nation around which all the European countries could be moved to the bargaining table to revise the Versailles settlement, which Welles saw as the source of Europe's current troubles. Italy would serve both as a conduit for communication between the Western democracies and Germany, as well as the example of what could be gained through negotiations. The appeasement of Italy would be the mechanism which started the whole peace machinery moving.

In a July 1937 speech at the University of Virginia, Welles made it clear that the United States would welcome a general settlement to Europe's problems through a revision of the Versailles treaty. The treaty, Welles declared, had left Germany with intolerable "moral and material burdens."[53] In a national radio speech that same month, Welles stated that "the causes of the ills from which the world suffers today revolve primarily about the fundamental fact that the injustices and maladjustments resulting from the Great War have never yet been rectified."[54] German revisionist demands, therefore, had some legitimacy and a way had to be found to satisfy them. Italy appeared to be the route as Roosevelt began to consider plans for an international conference.

In July, Welles got Roosevelt to send a belated reply to Mussolini's well-wishes on his 1936 reelection. Welles's move was prompted by a series of reports from Italy that indicated Mussolini's desire for an international conference to discuss ways to maintain peace in Europe. In April, Phillips reported that Mussolini had declared that "peace is absolutely essential for Italy," and that the Italians would support a disarmament conference called for by the United States.[55] In May, in an interview with the foreign editor of the

Scripps-Howard newspapers, William Simms, Mussolini stated that "if President Roosevelt would take the initiative and call an arms limitation conference in the near future the move would meet with great success." If no action was taken soon, however, war in Europe would result. Mussolini concluded that "Italy wants peace. She needs peace for a long time in which to develop the resources now at her command." Phillips's assessment was that Italy was committed to a "policy of peace and cooperation."[56] Welles informed the Italian ambassador, Augusto Rosso, that he thought Mussolini's comments were very important and were being considered by the United States.[57]

In his letter Roosevelt outlined his and Welles's thoughts on a mechanism for European peace. Roosevelt explained that his long delay in writing was because he had hoped "that the world situation would clarify sufficiently for me to discuss with you measures looking toward the stabilization of peace among nations." The president was "confident that you share with me the desire to turn the course of the world toward stabilizing peace. I have often wished that I might talk with you frankly and in person because from such a meeting great good might come." What was necessary, according to Roosevelt, was for the leading powers to reach a disarmament agreement and find effective means to increase international trade. "The two things must go hand in hand. It seems clear to me that if the nations can agree on armament reduction, even if it be in the form of a progressive reduction over a period of years, they can far more effectively discuss practical instruments for reduction of trade barriers, thus building up employment in industry to take the place of employment in armament."

The president even hinted at concessions for Italy when he added that "I recognize that as a part of the discussion of increasing trade, every consideration should be given to a more ready access to raw materials' markets for those nations which in themselves do not produce the raw materials necessary to industry."[58] The barrier of the Italo-Ethiopian war was removed and the main components of Roosevelt's and Welles's appeasement policy of late 1937 and 1938 had been formed and the necessity of Italy's cooperation for its success made clear.

Italy responded positively to Roosevelt's approach. In September, Foreign Minister Galeazzo Ciano, who both Phillips and Welles liked and respected, assured Phillips on the eve of his return visit to the United States that Italy would support any presidential peace effort. Ciano wanted Phillips to inform Roosevelt "that the Italian government would view with the utmost sympathy any effort made by the President to assure European peace and should the President be able to take the initiative, Italy would do everything in her power to lend her support."[59]

In October, Roosevelt adopted Welles's idea for peace. It consisted of the United States calling a world conference along the lines Roosevelt had described to Mussolini in July. In a lengthy memorandum for the president, Welles outlined his objectives and reasons for the conference. It was necessary that nations reach an agreement on how they "may obtain the right to have access upon equal and effective terms to raw materials and other elements necessary for their economic life." This would necessitate a revision of the Versailles treaty. As Welles pointed out, "Before the foundations of a lasting peace can be secured, international adjustments of various kinds may be found in order to remove those inequities which exist by reason of the nature of certain settlements reached at the termination of the Great War."[60]

As Welles later recalled, the general aim was an "understanding between this country and the leading powers of Europe to achieve economic cooperation." The conference would help create "an ultimate international economy based upon reduced armaments, a greater common use of world resources, and the improvement and simplification of economic relations" among nations.[61]

The first attempt to implement Welles's plan was blocked by Secretary Hull, who did not want Roosevelt taking the initiative in European affairs.[62] But Welles revived the idea in January and secured the secretary of state's agreement so long as Roosevelt first advised the British of Welles's plan. Again, central to the idea was an economic reordering of world trade. "It is my belief," Welles wrote Roosevelt, "that the proposal in itself will lend support and impetus to the effort of Great Britain, supported by France, to reach the basis for a practical understanding with Germany both on colonies and upon security, as well as upon European adjustments."[63] On January 11, Welles advised the British ambassador, Sir Ronald Lindsay, of his plan. Despite the endorsement of the British Foreign Office, Prime Minister Neville Chamberlain rejected the proposal because, he argued, it would interfere with his own appeasement efforts currently being negotiated with Italy and Germany.[64]

Roosevelt and Welles were upset by Chamberlain's rejection and his apparent decision to exclude the United States from participating in a settlement. American leaders believed that a general settlement had to be reached on Europe's problems, while Chamberlain pursued a bilateral and piecemeal approach of political and territorial adjustments with Germany and Italy. As the prime minister informed Roosevelt when he turned down the president's offer calling for a world conference, it would "delay consideration of specific points which must be settled if appeasement is to be achieved."[65]

In particular, American officials worried about negotiations being conducted with Italy. Roosevelt and Welles feared that the British were going to give away the lever of recognition of Ethiopia without receiving any settlement to other problems. As Roosevelt noted in his reply to Chamberlain, one concern was over the "harmful effect" *de jure* recognition of Italy's empire would have upon "the course of Japan" in China. Moreover, Roosevelt believed that although the recognition of Italy's conquest was inevitable, recognition should be granted only as part of securing Mussolini's assistance in reaching a general European settlement. "The recognition of the conquest of Ethiopia," Roosevelt wrote, "which at some appropriate time may have to be regarded as an accomplished fact, would seem to me to be a matter which affects all nations which are committed to the principles of nonrecognition and which should be dealt with as an integral part of measures for world appeasement."[66]

Welles informed Ambassador Lindsay that the recognition of Italy's empire was "an unpleasant pill which we should both swallow" in order to obtain Mussolini's aid in a settlement, but that Roosevelt wished that "we should both swallow it together."[67] Chamberlain, finally persuaded by Foreign Minister Anthony Eden, decided to delay his talks with Italy and reopen discussions with the United States. However, rapidly changing events on the continent, culminating in Hitler's annexation of Austria on March 12, 1938, brought an end to any discussions of peace based upon Welles's plan.

In the wake of the *Anschluss*, Chamberlain reopened negotiations with Mussolini. By the end of March, Britain had reached an agreement with Italy which traded *de jure* recognition of Italy's control of Ethiopia for the removal of Italian forces from Spain. The prime minister believed this was a major achievement in weakening the relationship between Rome and Berlin. The British Foreign Office pressed the United States for approval of its actions.

Welles, supported by the views of William Phillips, urged Roosevelt to issue a public statement in support of the British in order to aid in their effort at keeping Mussolini out of Hitler's orbit. Phillips believed that because the *Anschluss* was so unpopular in Italy and Germany was so distrusted by the Italians, it was quite possible to permanently divide Mussolini from Hitler.[68] Welles, his faith in Mussolini and the use of Italy as the road to peace unbroken, saw any move which would weaken the Axis as one that the United States had to support. On April 19, the president released a statement that the United States had "urged the promotion of peace through the finding of means for economic appeasement" and that it viewed the Anglo-Italian agreement with "sympathetic interest because it is proof of the value of peaceful negotiations."[69]

During the Sudetenland crisis, Roosevelt and Welles again turned to Mussolini. On September 27, 1938, Roosevelt wrote the Italian dictator that "I feel sure that you will agree with me as to the destructive and tragic effects of a war in Europe." Roosevelt asked Mussolini to "extend [his] help in the continuation of the efforts to arrive at an agreement of the questions at issue by negotiation."[70] American officials generally believed, as Ambassador Phillips stated, that "there was no doubt that the Duce played a strong hand at this critical moment" in bringing about the Munich conference and avoiding war.[71] This led Sumner Welles to declare in a radio speech on October 3 that because of Munich "today . . . more than at any time during the past two decades, there is presented the opportunity for the establishment by the nations of the world of a new world order based upon justice and upon law."[72]

Welles and Roosevelt's meeting with the new Italian ambassador, Prince Ascanio Colonna, on March 22, 1939, demonstrated both the persistence and the depth of their view that Mussolini held, in Roosevelt's words, the "key to peace."[73] The president began his meeting with the Italian ambassador by impressing upon him first that American resources and materials would be available to those who opposed Germany, and second that American opposition to Germany did not stem from an ideological opposition to the fact that it was ruled by a dictator.

Roosevelt then turned to his main objective for this meeting, to persuade Mussolini's ambassador that the Italian dictator held the key to peace in Europe, and that Italy could expect benefits from the United States if it was successful in helping to bring that about. Mussolini, the president declared, has "a very great opportunity presented to him today to prevent the world from being thrown into war." Hitler only intended to use Italy for his own advantages and "he would undoubtedly throw over Mussolini at any moment that seemed to him expedient." Thus, Roosevelt concluded, Mussolini should realize that he could serve both Italy's interests as well as those of the rest of the world if he would call for an international conference for peace.

Roosevelt assured the ambassador that the United States would participate and "that he himself . . . would lend his support to the finding of a reasonable solution to Europe's problems." Moreover, Mussolini "would not only be counted responsible for averting the outbreak of a European war" by arranging a conference, "but would also have the opportunity to gain any just concessions which he believed essential" for Italy's well-being. Finally, Roosevelt

told Prince Colonna that he regretted that he had never had the
opportunity of meeting Mussolini personally for an exchange of
opinions on world affairs, since he "believed that they would find
that they 'spoke the same language.' "[74]
In summary, the Italian invasion of Ethiopia failed to shake the
prevailing favorable analysis of Mussolini and fascism held by
Roosevelt and the State Department. Once the crisis of the Italo-
Ethiopian war had passed, good relations with Rome were re-
stored. The United States did not, as other studies on U.S.–Italian
relations have argued, adopt an anti-Fascist policy. Instead, Roosevelt, following the advice of Sumner Welles, proposed a peace
plan in which Italy played a key role in an overall European
settlement. The appeasement of Rome was considered essential if
there was to be any solution to the problem of Germany.

NOTES

    1. On American appeasement and Germany see Arnold A. Offner, *Ameri-
can Appeasement: United States Foreign Policy and Germany, 1933–1938*
(New York: W. W. Norton, 1968); Offner, "Appeasement Revisited: The
United States, Great Britain, and Germany, 1933–1940," *Journal of American
History* 64, no. 2 (September 1977): 373–93; C. A. MacDonald, *The United
States, Britain and Appeasement, 1936–1939* (New York: St. Martin's Press,
1981); Richard A. Harrison, "Appeasement and Isolation: The Relationship of
British and American Foreign Policies, 1935–1938" (Ph.D. diss., Princeton
University, 1974); William V. Wallace, "Roosevelt and British Appeasement
in 1938," *Bulletin-British Association for American Studies* 5 (1962): 4–30;
Hans-Jurgen Schröder, "The Ambiguities of Appeasement: Great Britain, the
United States and Germany, 1937–39," in Wolfgang J. Mommsen and Lothar
Kettenacker, eds., *The Fascist Challenge and the Policy of Appeasement* (Lon-
don: George Allen and Unwin, 1983); Patrick J. Hearden, *Roosevelt Confronts
Hitler: America's Entry into World War II* (DeKalb: Northern Illinois Univer-
sity Press, 1987).
    2. See David F. Schmitz, *The United States and Fascist Italy, 1922–1940*
(Chapel Hill: University of North Carolina Press, 1988), chaps. 2–6 for a
complete discussion of American foreign policy toward Mussolini prior to the
Italo-Ethiopian war.
    3. Brice Harris, Jr., *The United States and the Italo-Ethiopian Crisis* (Stan-

ford: Stanford University Press, 1964); John P. Diggins, *Mussolini and Fascism: The View from America* (Princeton, N.J.: Princeton University Press, 1972); Louis De Santi, "United States Relations with Italy under Mussolini, 1922–1941" (Ph.D. diss., Columbia University, 1951); Henderson B. Braddick, "A New Look at American Policy during the Italo-Ethiopian Crisis, 1935–1936," *Journal of Modern History* 34 (1962): 64–73; Robert A. Friedlander, "New Light on the Anglo-American Reaction to the Ethiopian War, 1935–1936," *Mid-America* 45 (1963): 115–25; and Rolfe G. Buzzell, "The Eagle and the Fasces: The United States and Italy, 1935–1939" (Ph.D. diss., University of California, Santa Barbara, 1977).

4. Robert Divine, *The Reluctant Belligerent* (New York: Wiley, 1979); John E. Wiltz, *From Isolation to War, 1931–1941* (New York: Crowell, 1968); Howard Jablon, *Crossroads of Decision: The State Department and Foreign Policy, 1933–1937* (Lexington: University of Kentucky Press, 1983); and Robert Dallek, *Franklin D. Roosevelt and American Foreign Policy, 1932–1945* (New York: Oxford University Press, 1979).

5. Braddick, "New Look," and Friedlander, "New Light."

6. Braddick, "New Look," p. 67.

7. Ibid., pp. 64, 71.

8. Harris, *Italo-Ethiopian Crisis*, p. v.

9. Ibid., p. 64.

10. De Santi, "United States," p. 260.

11. Diggins, *Mussolini and Fascism*, pp. 290–92, 304–5.

12. Buzzell, "Eagle and the Fasces," pp. vi, viii–ix.

13. William L. Langer and S. Everett Gleason, *The Challenge to Isolation: The World Crisis of 1937–1940 and American Foreign Policy*, 2 vols. (New York: Harper and Row, 1964).

14. Dallek, *Franklin D. Roosevelt*.

15. For example, Offner in *American Appeasement* does not investigate the perceptions American policymakers held of fascism as an ideology. Consequently, he neither considers the prior experience policymakers had with Mussolini as a factor in the development of American policy toward Hitler, nor does he see Italy playing a significant role in America's appeasement policy. MacDonald in *United States, Britain and Appeasement* argues that the Roosevelt administration sought to pressure Germany into abandoning its autarchic economic policies as part of an overall American policy to establish the Open Door as the basis for European peace. To do this, American policy sought to strengthen the position of German "moderates" in the Nazi government. But MacDonald fails to note that the analysis of a split between "moderates" and "extremists" was first developed with regard to Italy. The influence of the prior Italian experience is obvious yet overlooked. Hearden in *Roosevelt Confronts Hitler* argues that the United States saw Germany "as a dangerous have-not country which threatened both American prosperity and European tranquility."

But Hearden sees American policy as mainly antagonistic with Germany and underestimates the sincerity with which policymakers believed that an appeasement of Germany could be reached, based upon the prior experience of good relations with Italy.

16. Henry L. Stimson and McGeorge Bundy, *On Active Service in Peace and War* (New York: Harper and Brothers, 1947), pp. 268–70.

17. Schmitz, *United States and Fascist Italy.*

18. Roosevelt to Long, June 16, 1933, Box 105 Breckinridge Long Papers, Library of Congress (hereafter cited as BLP).

19. Roosevelt to Long, September 11, 1933, Box 105 BLP.

20. William Phillips Diary, August 14, 1934, William Phillips Papers, Houghton Library, Harvard University (hereafter cited as WPP).

21. "Italy" State Department Information Series No. 67, February 4, 1935, Record Group 59, National Archives, Washington, D.C. (hereafter cited as NA RG59), 865.00/1713.

22. Roosevelt to Long, March 9, 1935, Box 114 BLP.

23. Long to Roosevelt, April 5, 1935, PSF: Breckinridge Long, Franklin D. Roosevelt Papers, Franklin D. Roosevelt Library, Hyde Park, New York (hereafter cited as Roosevelt Papers).

24. Edgar B. Nixon, ed., *Franklin D. Roosevelt and Foreign Affairs*, 3 vols. (Cambridge, Mass.: Belknap Press of Harvard University Press, 1969), vol. 3, pp. 12–14.

25. Samuel Rosenman, ed., *The Public Papers and Addresses of Franklin D. Roosevelt*, 13 vols. (New York: Random House, 1938–1950), vol. 4, pp. 442–43.

26. Roosevelt to Straus, February 13, 1936, PSF: Diplomatic Box 42, Roosevelt Papers.

27. Cordell Hull, *The Memoirs of Cordell Hull*, 2 vols. (New York: Macmillan, 1948), vol. 1, p. 421.

28. For examples, see *Foreign Relations of the United States: Diplomatic Papers*, vol. 2 (1934), pp. 754–57 (hereafter cited as *FRUS* followed by year and volume); Long to Roosevelt, February 15, 1935, February 21, 1935, April 5, 1935, April 19, 1935, November 29, 1935; Roosevelt to Long, May 8, 1935, all PSF: Breckinridge Long, Roosevelt Papers; Long to Hull, March 6, 1935, 765.84/216, September 24, 1935, 765.84/1342, October 18, 1935, 765.84/2245, all NA RG59.

29. Long to Roosevelt, April 19, 1935, PSF: Breckinridge Long, Roosevelt Papers.

30. See note 28; Harris, *Italo-Ethiopian Crisis*, p. 31.

31. Mary Millsap, "Mussolini and the United States" (Ph.D. diss., University of California, Los Angeles, 1972), pp. 8–9.

32. Moffat to Dunn, January 3, 1936, Moffat to Castle, February 28, 1936, vol. 10, J. Pierrepont Moffat Papers, Houghton Library, Harvard University.

33. William Phillips, *Ventures in Diplomacy* (Boston: Beacon Press, 1952), p. 168.

34. *FRUS* 1935 I, pp. 723–25.

35. Ibid., p. 729.

36. Ibid., pp. 778–84.

37. Hull, *Memoirs* I, p. 422; Kirk to Hull, August 19, 1935, PSF: Italy 1933–38, Roosevelt Papers.

38. Roosevelt to Hull, October 4, 1935, Official File 547A, Roosevelt Papers.

39. Quoted in Robert Sherwood, *Roosevelt and Hopkins* (New York: Harper and Brothers, 1948), p. 79.

40. Jablon, *Crossroads of Decision*, pp. 108–9; Harris, *Italo-Ethiopian Crisis*, pp. 67–68; James MacGregor Burns, *Roosevelt: The Lion and the Fox* (New York: Harcourt, Brace, and World, 1956), p. 257.

41. Harris, *Italo-Ethiopian Crisis*, pp. 97–113.

42. *FRUS* 1935 I, pp. 826–33.

43. Donald B. Schewe, ed., *Franklin D. Roosevelt and Foreign Affairs*, 11 vols. (New York: Garland Press, 1979), vol. 1, document no. 11.

44. Phillips to Roosevelt, April 22, 1937, WPP.

45. Ibid.

46. Hugh R. Wilson, *Diplomat Between Wars* (New York:Longmans, Green, 1941), p. 323.

47. Quoted in Hugh DeSantis, *The Diplomacy of Silence* (Chicago: University of Chicago Press, 1983), p. 71.

48. "Italy: Political Estimate," June 30, 1937, NA RG59, 865.00/1745.

49. Phillips to Department, May 25, 1937, NA RG59, 711.652/95.

50. Hull to Phillips, June 19, 1937, NA RG59, 711/652/5.

51. Sayre to Phillips, November 19, 1937, NA RG59 711.652/119.

52. Hull to Phillips, November 26, 1937, NA RG59 711.652/126.

53. Quoted in MacDonald, *United States*, p. 31.

54. Frank Warren Graff, "The Strategy of Involvement: A Diplomatic Biography of Sumner Welles, 1933–1943" (Ph.D. diss., University of Michigan, 1971), p. 168.

55. Phillips to Roosevelt, April 22, 1937, WPP.

56. *FRUS* 1937 I, pp. 655–57.

57. Phillips Diary, May 28, 1937, WPP.

58. Schewe, ed., *Roosevelt and Foreign Affairs*, vol. 2, document no. 402.

59. *FRUS* 1937 I, pp. 121–22.

60. Ibid., pp. 665–70.

61. Sumner Welles, *The Time for Decision* (New York: Harper and Brothers, 1944), pp. 50, 65.

62. Hull, *Memoirs* I, pp. 546–49.

63. *FRUS* 1938 I, pp. 115–17.

64. Ibid., pp. 118–20.
65. Ibid.
66. Ibid., pp. 120–22.
67. Quoted in MacDonald, *United States*, p. 71.
68. Phillips Diary, April 4, 1938, WPP.
69. *FRUS* 1938 I, pp. 147–48.
70. Phillips, *Ventures in Diplomacy*, p. 221.
71. Ibid., p. 222; see also Phillips to Hull, October 7, 1938, October 21, 1938, NA RG38.
72. Graff, "Strategy of Involvement," p. 242.
73. Memorandum by Roosevelt, March 19, 1939, PSF: Italy, Phillips, Roosevelt Papers. This memorandum was drawn up by the president for his own use during his meeting with Ambassador Colonna.
74. *FRUS* 1939 II, pp. 620–22.

5

The United States and Great Britain: Presidential Diplomacy and Alternatives to Appeasement in the 1930s

Richard A. Harrison

Throughout the 1930s it was an article of faith among the most influential members of the British government that American foreign policy consisted entirely of empty words.[1] Since then, even sympathetic historians have tended to agree that Great Britain could not look across the Atlantic for meaningful support in confronting the expansionism of Germany, Italy, and Japan before World War II. To the extent that appeasement was a policy arising from the absence of alternatives, therefore, the behavior of the United States helped justify it.[2]

There is, however, a record of American initiatives in the thirties designed to keep appeasement—correction of the mistakes of the 1919 Versailles treaty—from degenerating into a policy of irresponsible surrender to the demands of aggressors. It lies in the personal and usually secret diplomacy of Franklin D. Roosevelt, which produced opportunities for Anglo-American cooperation in defense of the international system upon which the security and influence of both countries were based. London's refusal to recognize and respond to Roosevelt's overtures was the single most important reason his initiatives failed.

Partnership with Great Britain was the central objective of FDR's foreign policy and was crucial to his goals in the world, but it was his limitation of American commitments that most impressed the British. What Roosevelt envisioned as a prudent and constructive relationship providing for abundant mutual support, most leaders in London shunned as inadequate, unreliable, and provocative. They did not trust American objectives and many Britons, notably Neville Chamberlain, pursued appeasement as a way to achieve a European settlement free from American "meddling."[3]

Roosevelt's approach to Britain was fundamentally antagonistic to what appeasement had become by 1935. It was his sense that the peace to which all democratic leaders were devoted depended on the maintenance of a system in which aggression and the violation of treaties were not tolerated. While legitimate grievances had to be redressed before they led to war, it was essential that such changes comply with clear rules for the behavior of states in a world community. An orthodox Wilsonian, Roosevelt believed that the real interests of the United States were safe only in a "rational and peaceful international liberal order."[4]

FDR had learned from Wilson's failures. He harbored no ambition to police the world, but rather sought a consortium of great powers, each chiefly responsible for its own informal sphere of influence to provide collective leadership. That vision accepted the finitude of American interests and resources. It shaped his foreign policy from 1933 onward and was the basis of his "Four Policemen" proposal at the end of World War II. It assumed that conflicts among the great powers would be minimized by the separateness of their jurisdictions while they shared a dependence upon the system as a whole. Each could rely on the others to support its local authority, but the responsibility to exercise that authority remained its own. Roosevelt's frequent advice that Europeans look to his Good Neighbor Policy as a model, therefore, was to demonstrate his principles in practice.

Roosevelt looked for European leadership to which he could offer American support. The United States would never join the League of Nations, although FDR frequently considered reforming or even replacing the League to make American affiliation possible.[5] Meanwhile, if the member states fulfilled their obligations to the Covenant, he intended to back them, independently but as fully as possible. He looked first, though, to the individual governments for leadership, and above all to Great Britain. When British initiative was not forthcoming, he secretly promoted ideas of his own to stimulate assertive British policies that might elicit American cooperation.[6]

Since his suggestions often produced no such response, many of his most dramatic ideas were left undeveloped and unfulfilled. Regarded separately, they appear chaotic and vague.[7] Taken together, they form a consistent pattern that a few British policymakers eventually found persuasive. As crises multiplied, so did his proposals, but the British government insisted that the United States commit itself formally, if not always to taking the lead then at least to supporting specific British interests, before it would abandon appeasement.

Roosevelt could not make such a commitment, and the subtlety and indirection with which he often communicated his ideas did nothing to relieve London's anxiety. He was constrained by the anti-European, unilateralist sentiment of isolationism, greatly strengthened in the 1930s by revisionist criticisms of American involvement in the World War and by the Great Depression. Domestic recovery was Roosevelt's first concern, not least of all because without a sound domestic base he could exert no useful influence in the world. Yet his concentration on problems at home convinced Britons that his administration was selfishly nationalistic.[8]

Roosevelt opposed isolationism and appeasement because both left the initiative in world affairs to governments that were prepared to destroy the international order to get what they wanted. Yet he could not challenge isolationism directly. He intended to "educate" the American people gradually, and he used secret diplomacy that often infuriated and confused London to prevent a confrontation at home that might jeopardize the New Deal. His ingenious use of discretionary executive authority to provide independent support for collective security only seemed to confirm to the British that he could not change isolationism and that

Congress was the decisive branch in making American foreign policy.

British memories of American isolationism were long and unforgiving, and they commonly produced an active hostility toward the United States. They explain why British decision-makers demanded the commitments Roosevelt was unable to make, and why his failure to make them intensified the demands. Isolationist rhetoric often drowned out FDR's subtler internationalism, and insofar as the president had to shape his policy to domestic considerations, that policy was unlikely to inspire confidence in London. To Britons, American isolationism significantly limited their own options in the 1930s.

There was a pernicious symbiosis between appeasement and isolationism. Roosevelt knew that educating the American people meant overcoming the revisionist doctrine that all Europeans were equally untrustworthy. His adroit manipulation of American policy was undermined every time appeasement seemed to reward aggressors. The ideals and principles Americans held sacred, at least in the abstract, were intrinsic to popular attitudes about international affairs and to the exceptionalism on which isolationism was premised. Roosevelt's personal criteria for the proper international system also defined legitimate state behavior in typically American terms. Repetitious American appeals to principles put off British leaders who prided themselves on the "realism" of appeasement. But since they made outmoded assumptions about the "rational" behavior of states and leaders, their realism was much less applicable to the problems of the 1930s than was Roosevelt's concept of an international system in which those principles were effective. Because irresponsible appeasement was not only unsuccessful, but also, to most Americans, "wrong," it stigmatized the governments that practiced it and so sabotaged the president's efforts to combat isolationism.

At the beginning of Roosevelt's administration it seemed that his goals of educating the people, engineering recovery, and convincing Britain to trust and cooperate with him were mutually exclusive.[9] And leaving the details of foreign policy to the Department of State made things worse, for Roosevelt had little confidence in the professional diplomatic corps or in Secretary Cordell Hull. Although he was occasionally useful to FDR, Hull's difficult personality and his obsessive confidence that trade liberalization was the sole remedy for international tensions more often impeded the president's efforts. Thanks to Hull, Britons who feared American domination of world markets were especially prone to be wary of the administration.[10] While Hull believed policy should "follow after public opinion," and so was always influenced by isolationist arguments, Roosevelt meant to guide and shape that opinion to support his policy.[11]

Yet the president's unorthodox and highly personal approach to foreign policy caught the British so completely unprepared that at first they found it easier to deal with the State Department.[12] Roosevelt often spoke for himself, but he also used others to speak for him. He would communicate directly with governments—even the king—or he would employ an unexpecting visitor to carry important messages. He might call upon any department of government or member of his cabinet to make his points. There were also several people who, without his authority, claimed to speak on his behalf; and the State Department, which had the authority, often had no inkling what he wanted to say. Given the distrust already present in London, such unpredictability, and the experimental nature of many of FDR's ideas, tended to obscure his unflagging attempts to create an Anglo-American partnership.

Roosevelt ascribed the urgency of this partnership to the menace of Nazi Germany. He considered Hitler a madman, and throughout the decade he lectured visitors on the propensity of Germans to be bullies.[13] From his own school days in Germany he drew the lesson that the best way to make Germans behave in a civilized way was to stand up to their threats. It was a typically simple homily, the sort that exasperated sophisticated Britons; but it reflected Roosevelt's honest judgment of both Germany and appeasement.

While Roosevelt was primarily concerned about the danger of war in Europe, immediate American interests and the anti-European character of isolationism drew his attention to the Orient. He regarded Japan (and Italy) as less dangerous than Germany, but he assumed aggression had to be resisted whatever its source because the international system required consistent defense. Freer to act in Pacific affairs, he used differences with Japan to improve cooperation with London, whose own interests in the region were often in line with those of the United States. He sought to reassure the British that a firmer line against Hitler would not require them to confront Tokyo and Berlin together without American help.

Relying as he did on personal diplomacy, FDR put a premium on having direct access to leaders of the national government. Before his election he asked a British journalist to convey some of his ideas to a member of the cabinet, and he contemplated a pre-inaugural visit to Europe, where he hoped to spend most of his time in London. During that time he spoke at length with Ambassador Sir Ronald Lindsay, touching on the problems of recovery and disarmament that dominated international affairs in a way he hoped would convince Whitehall—the British government—of his enthusiasm for cooperation.[14] As always, Roosevelt's proposed solutions were suggestive rather than definitive. It was clear from the first, however, that the British were much more concerned with the details of "settlements" than they were with the nuances of cooperation. The awful problem of intergovernmental war debts illustrated the distance between their perspective and the president's.

Of the many grievances nursed by Britons, the war debts owed to the United States were the most infuriating and in substance the least important. From the messages he sent via Lindsay and other channels, it is clear that Roosevelt's greatest concern was the potential of the debts to inflame public opinion against closer relations with Britain, for their symbolic weight was all out of proportion to their economic significance. In June 1933 the Foreign Office counted war debts as the most serious problem in Anglo-American relations, but FDR regarded them as an overstated annoyance, to be set to rest as quickly as possible. He saw a "legal and a moral side" to the problem and was "not very much interested" in the legal side.[15] The answers he proposed were all directed at satisfying popular demands for fairness rather than at extracting the full measure in payment. Personally, he said, he wanted to cancel the debts completely, but since that would not have quelled popular demands for fairness, he wanted to ease the burden on the Europeans as much as he could.[16] All he asked of any proposal was that it satisfy the American people as to the good faith of the debtors, without which no government deserved American cooperation. He also wanted to use discussions of the debts to confront a broad range of economic and political issues that could greatly improve Anglo-American relations. Meanwhile, he would cultivate a friendly atmosphere, "[play] for time and [hope] that something [would] turn up."[17]

Roosevelt's flexibility was far from enough for the British. Not only did they deem the debts unjustified; they regarded American insistence on any substantial repayment as evidence that Washington was uncooperative and arrogant. By 1933, moreover, American subscription to the Lausanne formula linking debts and reparations was Britain's absolute prerequisite for a debt settlement, which in turn Britons declared necessary before other economic issues could be addressed. Roosevelt's musings about reducing the payments fell on deaf ears.[18]

Only because FDR insisted, Prime Minister J. Ramsay MacDonald visited him in Washington in the spring of 1933, and in their discussions Roosevelt continued to express his understanding, even support, of the British position. Nevertheless, he warned London that Congress was unlikely to give him authority to deal with the problem on his own, and although his exclusion of debts from the agenda of the upcoming World Economic Conference indicated no breakthrough in the near future, the British persuaded themselves that he had promised to obtain powers to negotiate a quick settlement.[19]

Whitehall soon realized that the tedious details of debt negotiations were much less important to Roosevelt than they were to either London or the State Department. When he encountered problems with Congress, Roosevelt almost casually invited the British to make token partial payments of the installments of June and December 1933, promising on his own authority to certify that no default had occurred. There was endless dickering and no little discomfort in London, several rounds of negotiations opened and closed, but in the end the partial payments were made, Roosevelt absolved Britain of default, and gradually there developed a routine in making as little as possible of the issue on both sides.[20] What concerned Roosevelt throughout this process was that, by insisting on the outright cancellation of obligations that were, whatever their faults, completely legal, and by offering token payments that were too small to impress American opinion, London was impeding his efforts to bring Congress and the people with him into world affairs.

In the spring of 1934 Congress reacted to the absence of a settlement by passing the Johnson Act, forcing debtors to choose between full installment payments or default. Whitehall's response was predictably bitter, and the Foreign Office threw up its hands at the "impotence of [the] President and [the] obstinancy of Congress."[21] In spite of the new law FDR declared that the British were not already in default because of their token payments, a statement whose logic Lindsay found "astonishing" and whose intention British experts understood to be "helpful." But the national government refused to reciprocate by continuing token payments if default was now unavoidable in any case.[22]

Default had always been unavoidable, given the British position and the realities of American politics. Roosevelt's hopes for some other outcome required, first, that London as the debtor initiate any new ideas and, second, that while a settlement could reduce the amount of the debt dramatically, it had to be "realistic." Seeing the impasse, he made the process of defaulting as painless for both sides as he could. War debts continued to crop up in lists of Anglo-American differences throughout the thirties,[23] but the issue had effectively been defused by 1934. It did not again make any significant impact on the policies of London or Washington.

Its legacy, though, was that British leaders resented the United States all the more. Roosevelt's failure to ask for power to cancel the debts rankled especially. A notable characteristic of attitudes

among Britons toward the United States was their failure to understand how American politics affected the president. FDR's original
and exploratory ideas for dealing with the debts had been rejected
in London as "haphazard and . . . contradictory." His casual han-
dling of the arcane details as he concentrated on improving Anglo-
American relations generally was taken as evidence of his
"ignorance." Throughout, his emphasis was on the "necessity of
conserving good relations between the British Empire and the
United States so that they should stand together to deal with any
crisis that might arise," and specifically to reduce Britain's war
debt obligations so that resources could be devoted to prepare for
such a crisis.[24] Sir Frederick Leith-Ross, chief economic adviser
to the government and London's primary negotiator on war debts,
understood that default, however painful, was at least the end of
the problem.[25] To many of his colleagues, however, the very use
of the word made the problem infinitely worse.

Other economic issues also generated tensions. For example, the
administration's early "nationalistic" domestic program delayed
any agreement on currency stabilization long enough to produce
ill feelings in London. After the initial phase of the New Deal was
past, Roosevelt used stabilization talks to build confidence and
open important channels of communication, and then his unorthodox methods and inveterate empiricism only aggravated British
leaders who were more interested in the details of the problem than
in a long-term partnership.

Roosevelt's original approach to stabilization was superficial,
in part because he did not, as the British quickly noted, understand
the problem,[26] and in part because he was preoccupied with
American recovery. His uncertain monetary policy in the spring
of 1933 offered little prospect for a stabilization accord at the
World Economic Conference that summer. Roosevelt had already
barred war debts from the agenda and British experts doubted the
chances for any improvement of international trade. They therefore placed great emphasis on currency stabilization as the major
project for the conference, believing it would help "develop the
cordial co-operation of Great Britain and the United States" FDR

said he wanted.[27] But before the conference met the president
adopted a unilateralist approach to the economic crisis that was not
amenable to international cooperation, and stabilization, which
might have served British interests, held no attraction for him in
1933.[28]

FDR's disinterest in stabilization was expedient and temporary.
His famous message to the Economic Conference, a clumsy and
intemperate refusal to join in stabilization at that time, accorded
with his immediate priorities, but it caught the British unprepared.
Already distressed at Roosevelt's limitations on the conference
agenda, they exploded at this new affront. MacDonald and Chancellor of the Exchequer Chamberlain, who identified their own
reputations with the success of the conference, took FDR's attitude
as a personal insult, and the level of anger at the United States in
London was higher in July 1933 than it had been in years.[29]
Chamberlain thereafter considered FDR no more than an "opportunistic politician . . . an amateur and a medicine man . . . [for
whom] the rest of the world can go hang."[30] To Sir Robert
Vansittart, permanent under secretary of state at the Foreign Office, Roosevelt's behavior was "nauseatingly disloyal" and consistent with the "precipitate egotism" that had marked American
policy since 1919.[31]

The issue was poisonous because London put a much higher
premium on stabilization than did the president, and Roosevelt was
especially truculent because his opponents at home tended to take
the British point of view. By 1935, however, tempers had had time
to cool in Whitehall, the United States had emerged from the most
desperate period of the depression, and most important, international tensions were emphasizing the need for Anglo-American
cooperation. Stabilization could be discussed once again, but as
usual the specifics of the issue were never as important to FDR as
the development of a habit of working together.

That spring, the convenient topic to begin discussions was
exchange equalization funds. Roosevelt, through Treasury Secretary Henry Morgenthau, Jr., gently suggested that the two governments share information to achieve an informal stabilization of the

dollar with the pound. Led by Chamberlain, whose wholly negative view of the United States had not changed at all, London
rejected the suggestion in a tone calculated to echo the insult in
Roosevelt's message to the Economic Conference. There was disagreement over this in the British government, but the chancellor's
influence on the issue was as complete as the contempt for Americans that came across in his message. The president henceforth
expected only the worst from Chamberlain.[32]

There was no progress on this unpromising beginning for more
than a year, during which British policymakers divided over the
wisdom of cultivating Washington's goodwill. Sir Warren Fisher,
Vansittart's counterpart at the Treasury, saw in stabilization a
chance to help shape the future direction of American policy.
While most of his colleagues simply lamented the influence of the
isolationists, he understood that positive responses to Roosevelt's
incomplete proposals might enable the president to counter that
influence.[33]

This sounded less like Chamberlain's Treasury than Anthony
Eden's Foreign Office, where officials tended to be much more
interested in cooperation with Washington. Ambassador Lindsay,
of course, was especially anxious on that point, particularly as he
knew that it was Roosevelt personally who was pressing stabilization. Given the president's notorious disinterest in such topics, the
ambassador saw that matters of much higher policy were involved.[34] Differences between the British Treasury and Foreign
Office mirrored differences between the State Department and
Treasury in Washington. There it was Morgenthau, much closer
than Hull to FDR, who was often the eager agent of presidential
diplomacy, and stabilization discussions marked his emergence in
that role.

A financial crisis in France in 1936 renewed Morgenthau's
approach to London. In an atmosphere of deepening international
danger, there was less subtlety this time. Morgenthau declared his
intention to establish a "channel of communication" to deal with far
more than immediate currency problems. In spite of Chamberlain's
obvious reservations, Morgenthau and the Foreign Office finally

carried the point, establishing formal treasury-to-treasury contacts that gave Roosevelt a direct line into the British government without going through he State Department. When the French finally appealed for help in their crisis, therefore, the United States and Britain were prepared to act effectively, quickly, and together to produce a tripartite stabilization agreement that especially pleased Morgenthau because it worked against German interests and ambitions. Over Hull's strong objections and in accordance with the president's intentions, that was the point he wanted to stress.[35]

In dealing with currencies and debts, Roosevelt craved no specific agreement as much as he wanted to establish mutual confidence and mutual interests. Commercial relations between the two countries were likewise valuable to him chiefly as an avenue to partnership, and so he tended to regard the details of trade negotiations as minor obstacles. Unlike other issues, however, Anglo-American trade had substantial importance in its own right, and it was burdened by serious problems that not even careful diplomacy, let alone FDR's virtuoso technique, could overcome. For most of the thirties FDR gave Hull free rein on trade negotiations, and the secretary undertook the job with the zeal of a monomaniac. For volume, intensity, and visibility, no other American initiatives of the decade could match Hull's pursuit of liberalized trade. It is not surprising that historians have mistaken his energetic work for the primary thrust of American policy before the war.

Generally, Roosevelt sympathized with Hull's goals. While he objected to Britain's Imperial Preference system less hotly than did the secretary, he too wanted to increase American exports to the empire.[36] Shortly after his inauguration he had Norman H. Davis, his frequent ambassador-at-large, propose a tripartite trade consortium among the United States, Britain, and Canada, the real purpose of which was to pave the way for a cooperative economic policy. The proposal failed then and again in 1934, for the British naturally regarded it as hostile to their imperial commercial regime.[37]

Hull's strategy was to preach the merits of lower trade barriers and to call upon other governments to agree with his principles.

London saw too many pitfalls in American commercial policy to
anticipate real progress, but the "political implications" of an
agreement with the United States were so attractive that Foreign
Secretary Sir Samuel Hoare finally proclaimed British sympathy
for Hull's objectives soon after the beginning of the Italo-Ethiopian
war.[38]

To Hull, the Italian aggression—which he blamed entirely on
Italy's need for markets—confirmed that trade agreements would
solve the world's problems. Davis, who was also the secretary's
old friend, offered a similar analysis of German policy.[39] Such an
obsessively narrow interpretation began to erode Hull's credibility, and thus the impact of his appeals, in both London and
Washington, a process accelerated by the secretary's reliance on
excruciating monologues to make his points.[40]

When the potential political advantages of a trade treaty were
emphasized by others, however, most Britons paid closer attention,
although Chamberlain was not yet interested in an agreement.
Typically, he cited the technical impediments to a pact and paid
mere lip service to its broader implications. Not until Roosevelt's
reelection, which coincided with the accelerated deterioration of
the world order, did London agree, in principle, to begin informal
discussions.[41] This came, however, on the eve of Chamberlain's
succession to the premiership, an event anticipated gloomily in the
State Department. As Ambassador Robert W. Bingham in London
noted, "the purely financial mind in any country is without the
quality of vision."[42]

Roosevelt demonstrated the political implications of trade with
his most important contribution to the commercial negotiations, an
invitation to Walter Runciman, president of the Board of Trade in
the British cabinet, to visit Washington. Why Runciman came was
secret, apparently even from Hull, who used the Briton as a
sounding board for several extended monologues on liberalization.
Private conversation with Roosevelt, however, covered much more
colorful terrain. "Fiscal questions," Runciman reported to Prime
Minister Stanley Baldwin, "are not the chief interest of the President and it is only in connection with . . . the maintenance of peace

that he discusses these questions at all."[43] In those meetings in January 1937, FDR also offered suggestions for joint Anglo-American policies to check Japanese expansion and urged intimate military and naval cooperation between Washington and London.[44] Runciman, whom the State Department had labeled a foe of a trade agreement, returned home as a champion of the negotiations.

Encouraged by Runciman's report and by other indications that Roosevelt wanted an agreement to facilitate better relations across the board, the Foreign Office took up the cause of a trade treaty with renewed vigor in 1937. Although he often said that he was sympathetic, Chamberlain was the main obstacle to progress. His occasionally contradictory explanations for his own policy[45] indicated that he was finding excuses to postpone any new agreements, and thus that he was still reluctant to get involved with the United States. By early 1938 he had maneuvered Eden and Runciman, the cabinet members most committed to a trade pact, out of their positions, had used commercial differences with Washington to explain his disinclination to accept Roosevelt's invitation to visit the United States, and had embarked upon an appeasement initiative toward Italy and Germany that alienated the president. Not until after Munich did the trade negotiations produce a treaty, by which time its impact on world events was negligible.

Roosevelt had encouraged Hull but had never shared his faith that freer commerce was a panacea. "These trade treaties are just too goddamned slow," he told Morgenthau after Munich. "The world is moving too fast."[46] He expected no more of debt settlements or currency stabilization, for as he wrote in 1937, "The more I study the situation the more I am convinced that an economic approach to peace is a pretty weak reed."[47] His most important efforts for peace and Anglo-American solidarity concerned political and even military questions to which, in spite of isolationism, his response was increasingly assertive and imaginative. He had said before his election that it would be his "single minded purpose" to achieve "a complete identity of political and economic interests" among the United States, Britain, and Canada,[48] and for all the apparent digressions in his policy he never wavered from that objective.

One of the few international issues in which the American people evinced real interest after the World War was disarmament, and so FDR used it to demonstrate his cooperative intentions. In his first conversation with Lindsay he spoke of the connection between recovery and reducing arms expenditures, and then tossed out a list of exploratory proposals for limiting weapons. In his meetings with European leaders in 1933, however, he played down the importance of real disarmament by the democracies because of the Nazi menace.[49] American politics might demand a certain fidelity to the ideal of disarmament, but Roosevelt never let that obscure the need for enforceable collective security.

The British conditioned their participation in any disarmament agreement on the willingness of the United States to cooperate in its enforcement. This was a recurring theme of British policy during the thirties, and FDR recognized that American cooperation with collective action would significantly enhance European security. The State Department and his advisers wanted the Geneva Disarmament Conference to focus on regional pacts, simply excluding an obstinate Japan in order to make some headway in Europe. But to Roosevelt that approach seemed likely to encourage Japanese militarism. Even worse, it would officially separate the United States from any European settlement. To the horror of professional diplomats, therefore, in May 1933 he embraced Prime Minister MacDonald's imperfect plan for a global disarmament agreement because he believed it was perfectible and because it was his purpose to encourage British leadership. He also pledged that the United States would not interfere with collective action against an aggressor, carefully reserving the independent right to decide if such action was warranted and declining to make the pledge in a form that required Senate ratification. He also called for a nonaggression pact in which the definition of an aggressor would be as unambiguous as possible. Davis repeated his proposals at Geneva. All of this he timed to precede a speech by Hitler that was expected to exacerbate growing tensions over German policy, and thus he offered some salvation to what seemed a dying disarmament conference. While it never directly challenged isolationism, his initiative went far to satisfy the European democracies so they could fulfill their own responsibilities, further encouraged by FDR's unmistakable opposition to German rearmament.[50]

There were reservations aplenty in London about the nonaggression pact, but by and large the British welcomed Roosevelt's ideas. Politicians and editorial writers shared a sense that the era of American indifference was over, and the president made them even happier by agreeing in private to certain British requirements in defining the "offensive" weapons he hoped to proscribe.[51] Then the isolationists on the Senate Foreign Relations Committee approved an amendment to require a mandatory and impartial arms embargo as part of American neutrality in any war, a measure that would prevent Roosevelt from supporting collective measures to punish aggressors, and so contradicted the pledges he and Davis had made. The president managed to smother it that spring, but its very appearance so alarmed the British that it nullified the impact of his proposal.[52]

The result was a gradual retreat by London from any commitment to enforce a disarmament agreement. Roosevelt repeated his pledge at the end of 1933 and waited for an opportunity to do more to bring the United States closer to collective security,[53] but Whitehall's attention was now on the unreliability of the Americans. The point of British policy by 1934 was to avoid having to respond to violations, and for this the absence of a contractual American commitment, while not the reason, was the preferred explanation. Reiterations of Roosevelt's promises and his private assurances of support were thus received in London almost as nuisances. For Chamberlain, the absence of any formal tie to the United States opened the way to a new European order that would "limit [British] liabilities" by accommodating Germany.[54]

When public and private statements by British officials attacked American dependability, Roosevelt tried to reinforce his earlier pledges, even countermanding Hull's attempt to limit their scope. Angry that the English refused to take him seriously, and in a last ditch effort to save the collapsing Geneva conference in October 1934, he privately proposed a strategy for confronting Germany: sanctions in the form of an international boycott of all trade with the Third Reich, which he compared to a blockade without war. Although it was completely unacceptable to the Department of State, he put the idea aside only after Hitler officially withdrew his delegation from Geneva.[55]

Roosevelt was less interested in literal disarmament than in the unity of British and American policy, but when the Senate rejected his proposal to make the United States a member of the World Court in January 1935, his standing in England suffered another blow.[56] He repeated the plan for a peaceful blockade when Hitler annihilated what was left of the restrictions on German arms that spring, still hoping to jolt Britain into taking the lead against Germany. Instead, London agreed to the Anglo-German Naval Treaty of June. British leaders rejected any thought of sanctions, and especially those Roosevelt suggested, because they assumed that sanctions were synonymous with war.[57] Now their official acceptance of German rearmament confused and disheartened not only Roosevelt, but most American observers. It seemed to FDR that no government across the Atlantic, and he undoubtedly was thinking of the one in London, cared "a continental damn about what the United States thinks or does."[58]

By the time Italy invaded Ethiopia, Congress had enacted the Neutrality Act of 1935, which included a mandatory impartial arms embargo. To Britons who did not want to assume the risks of enforcing the Covenant, the law was an ideal excuse to reject effective sanctions. Those who took Roosevelt's previous assurances more seriously were a small minority. In fact, Roosevelt had not contested the law at least partly because it was limited to six months, and its even-handed application in this particular war would operate primarily against the aggressor.[59] Maintaining a formal independence from the League, he promulgated a "moral embargo" that also penalized Italy, thereby putting the United States in a position to cooperate with sanctions if they were imposed. FDR reasoned that the League's success in this crisis would encourage popular acceptance of a discriminatory embargo against aggressors when the law was revised, and thus would facilitate even more effective support for the democracies in the future. Although the British and other Europeans recognized his intentions and acknowledged in private the significance of his position,[60] London was more concerned that Mussolini not be driven into Hitler's arms and that war not be provoked over Ethiopia. British protestations of loyalty to the League were for domestic consumption during a national election, but the real character of English policy was revealed in the Hoare-Laval plan of December 1935, which not only ended forever the ability of the League to maintain peace, but also so offended American opinion that it prevented the revision of the neutrality law for which Roosevelt had hoped.[61] The absence of a formal American commitment to defend British interests was a primary rationalization for the appeasement of Italy. "Realistic" arguments for declining to confront the aggressor, most of which went unquestioned in London in spite of the flawed assumptions on which they were based, were smoke screens for the uncertainties and fears of British policymakers that Roosevelt's indirect assurances, and even his explicit confidential urging, could not overcome.[62]

    In Whitehall the failure of collective security in the Italo-Ethiopian War was consistently taken thereafter as proof that a robust response to aggression would always fail, an assumption saved from being too embarrassingly *post hoc* by the belief that the United States was largely to blame.[63] Obviously, Britain would join in no action against Germany after the remilitarization of the Rhineland. Indeed, from Roosevelt's point of view the likelihood of any useful British leadership, or of any useful leadership in Europe, was depressingly small. Thus, when Britain asserted itself at the outbreak of the Spanish Civil War by creating the Non-Intervention Committee (NIC) to confine the conflict to Spain, Roosevelt endorsed the policy in spite of his doubts in order to assure London that it could count on the United States. His call for another "moral embargo" in the absence of a statute that covered civil wars was also a way to show Whitehall that he, and not Congress, truly made American policy.

By mid-1936, however, Roosevelt was no longer content to await British action before he asserted American influence. He began to explore opportunities for independent initiatives, such as unilateral American action against Germany through trade restrictions. In conversations with English visitors he made remarkable suggestions for Anglo-American cooperation, including once again his idea of a "peaceful blockade" and exchanges of significant military and naval information. These were dismissed in London as "somewhat dangerously jejune," but the president's frequent repetition of them began to have some effect.[64] By August, when he said that he might summon a world peace conference, he had already tested that idea on a number of guests and correspondents.[65]

An American-led peace conference, which seems to have first been suggested to Roosevelt by a group of British statesmen in April 1933,[66] held several possible attractions. If it were convened ostensibly to discuss economic recovery or disarmament, rather than any specific political crisis, it would face relatively little isolationist opposition. As the summoning power the United States would be morally, even if not legally, bound to its resolutions; and more important, the governments that accepted those resolutions would incur a moral commitment to the United States. It was impossible to imagine very definite agreements emerging from such a meeting. Far more likely would be general resolutions on principles to which Americans could not object. For hard-boiled Europeans, such an outcome might seem useless, even counterproductive. But for Roosevelt it would be an extremely important first step toward the more concrete exertion of American influence.

If all powers accepted the principles and abided by them, the process of consultation under Washington's aegis would be wellbegun and could continue. If some powers, having pledged themselves to those principles, broke their promises by violating their treaty obligations or committing aggression, the difference between such outlaw states and other, peace-loving states would be too clear for American public opinion to ignore. Likewise, a refusal to attend the conference, or even more, a rejection by any conferee of the principles, would set those states apart. Isolationism assumed a general equality of corruption among foreign governments, and so these distinctions were essential to persuading the American people that their own interests were linked directly to cooperation with countries whose policies served the cause of peace. So long as isolationism was a significant check on Roosevelt's ability to play a part in world affairs, what might be called the "negative advantages" of even a failed conference appealed to his imagination.

One of Roosevelt's complementary objectives was finding a way to associate the United States directly with mechanisms of collective security. At first he considered closer ties to the League,[67] but as that organization declined he thought of creating a new international body in which Washington could play a leading role. A conference might help him along those lines as well. Perhaps most important, a conference would satisfy the president's eagerness to take a hand in world affairs. Supremely confident of his own persuasive ability, Roosevelt always sought personal meetings with British leaders to emphasize his willingness to back London's lead. His tendency to write directly to the king produced endless consternation in Whitehall, and when he asked to be invited to Canada in 1934 or offered to make a radio address to the British people in 1935 the national government suspected some sinister American plot against the Empire. Still, the British had to pay attention.[68]

Each of Roosevelt's initiatives during the 1930s anticipated some or all of the advantages he expected of a conference. Before a peaceful blockade was imposed, for example, Germany (or Italy or Japan, each of which was at one time or another the target of the scheme) would be offered a chance to subscribe to the correct principles of international conduct. Only when the bandit nation persisted in its banditry, and thus made itself a pariah, would collective action be undertaken.[69] That was clearly in FDR's mind in August 1936, as the dust from the Rhineland crisis settled and Great Britain scrambled to conclude regional settlements that would require concessions to potential aggressors.[70]

Although Roosevelt hastily disavowed his suggestion of a heads of states meeting during the election campaign, he repeated and embellished it in private discussions with Canadian leaders who communicated it to London. He then had his ambassador in Berlin send the same message via his British colleague.[71] Led by Eden, and now Vansittart as well, the Foreign Office saw promise in the president's scheme. Eden was in perfect tune with Roosevelt, recognizing that even if such a conference failed because of the dictator powers, "the process of educating world opinion (and particularly U.S. opinion) should be salutary."[72]

Having put the conference in British minds as one way the United States might contribute to a united democratic front, Roosevelt moved to bolster British confidence. He amended current regulations governing export sales of warplanes to facilitate British purchases, which encouraged feelers from London about additional military transactions. Further, he proposed a secret exchange with Britain of highly classified information on industrial mobilization, thus lending his support to the cabinet faction that favored rearmament as part of a firmer foreign policy.[73]

An imperial conference in May 1937, which would coincide with the coronation of a new king and the installation of Chamberlain as prime minister, made the early months of that year seem like a good time for Roosevelt to intensify his overtures to London. With the peace conference scheme still in his mind, he employed several "back channels" to make clear his willingness to take such a dramatic step if the British gave him the opportunity.[74]

He turned again to the Treasury Department to communicate with Chamberlain, who was still chancellor. As a foundation for a peace conference, and to justify not using regular diplomatic channels, he cited the economic dangers of the current arms race. Morgenthau sent a dramatic message to Chamberlain asking for his suggestions as to how to solve that problem.[75] Roosevelt undoubtedly expected an answer that would at least invite him to do something that might galvanize world attention, but Chamberlain did not agree that the situation was urgent enough to warrant American action, and he wanted no interference in his own plans to appease Italy and reach a regional *modus vivendi* with Japan. Even Eden did not refer to a conference in his draft of Chamberlain's answer, although he spoke independently to Davis in a vein that suggested something along that line. He exerted himself instead to preventing the official response from being so cold that it would alienate Roosevelt. In the end, Chamberlain's reply included no hint of any interest in the scheme FDR had been putting forward since August.[76]

That disappointing message was so devoid of inspiration that FDR turned it over to the State Department. Chamberlain's single concrete proposal was that the United States revise the Neutrality Act, which he and his allies had convinced themselves was a fundamental disability to Britain, although the Foreign Office and other cabinet members understood that Roosevelt would manipulate the embargo in Britain's favor if that became necessary. FDR had promised several times to obtain greater discretionary authority when the law was revised in 1937.[77] The result was the policy of cash and carry, applied at the president's discretion to a list of strategic materials he would define. While the arms embargo itself was not changed, the revision was conspicuously pro-British, as both the Foreign Office and angry American isolationists noted.[78] But the purpose of the law was to keep the United States out of war. In that it was not pro-British, and that was the feature by which Chamberlain was most impressed. He saw in it no reason to alter the course he had charted for appeasement.

Roosevelt persisted. By distinguishing publicly between British rearmament, which was acceptable, and rearmament by aggressors, which was not,[79] he tried to keep "disarmament" available for American cooperation without threatening the growth of England's military power. He apparently had Davis invite Chamberlain, or if he could not come, Eden, to Washington, but the prime minister had no intention of going or of letting the foreign secretary go.[80] By the summer of 1937, with British appeasement in full sail, FDR was discouraged. "The British tories are still tories," he declared, "and in spite of Eden's denial, want peace at a great price."[81]

The incident at Marco Polo Bridge made every plan to prevent war more urgent. Leaving Eden further behind, Chamberlain redoubled his overtures to Italy. He also proposed a joint policy with the United States in Asia that would leave the initiative to Washington, but he anticipated no substantial action.[82] Hull issued an anodyne declaration of principles to which he then demanded international agreement. The British found it an "utter waste of time," and it confirmed Roosevelt's decision to "take the ball in international relations" away from the secretary.[83] The president's response to events in Asia was to call for a "quarantine" of aggressors, which although undefined was clearly based on his "peaceful blockade," and then to work with Under Secretary of State Sumner Welles on a plan to activate his peace conference scheme. Hull's violent objections briefly put that to rest.[84]

In conversations with Lord Robert Cecil, whom he had invited to Washington in November, Roosevelt reverted to a more general formulation of the conference proposal. He also reiterated his suggestion of a quarantine. But he warned that Britain had to take the lead in cooperative measures to keep the peace in Europe, and that it must not try to force him into the lead in the Pacific.[85] There was no response from Whitehall, where the battle between Eden and the prime minister made cooperation with the United States less and less likely. The foreign secretary was particularly alarmed at the inadequacies of British rearmament and at Chamberlain's use of the panic among military leaders to justify appeasement in spite of the damage it would do to Anglo-American relations.[86] Eden must therefore have been heartened, as doubtless he was meant to be, when Roosevelt simultaneously initiated secret military conversations with Canada and called for an increase in the American defense budget.[87]

It was in response to Chamberlain's intensified efforts to come to terms with Italy and Germany, and in the wake of an escalation of the crisis in Asia, that Roosevelt finally proposed his peace conference plan directly to London in January 1938. Without consulting Eden, Chamberlain rejected it immediately. And though the foreign secretary eventually softened the tone of the rejection,

and even indicated that London would cooperate if the president
went ahead, Roosevelt took the original reaction as decisive.[88] He
had intended to sidetrack Chamberlain's suit of the dictators,
which was exactly why the prime minister rejected the idea, and
Eden's efforts could not disguise Chamberlain's purpose. Shelving
the plan did not indicate that Roosevelt had lost interest in something that had been at the front of his mind for nearly two years. It
merely showed that he did not want to venture into European
affairs unless Britain was prepared to bear its full share of the
responsibility.

Determined to secure a new era of peace, Chamberlain was
ready to offer Italy *de jure* recognition of the conquest of Ethiopia
and make substantial colonial concessions in Africa to the Reich.
Although those policies would offend the United States, he told
his cabinet that FDR approved his plans for appeasement. Eden,
who knew better, resigned before the end of February 1938. The
Anschluss forced Chamberlain to admit that at least part of the
plans on which he had based his rejection of Roosevelt's proposal
had failed. But the Easter Pact with Italy, while it ultimately proved
empty, buoyed the prime minister's confidence in appeasement
and so helped maintain the distance between him and FDR. In
considering who should represent Britain in Washington when
Lindsay retired, Chamberlain declared "that as the Americans are
so rotten . . . it does not matter . . . who we send."[89]

It was during the Munich crisis that Roosevelt last proposed an
American-led peace conference. He also proposed much more
definite ways to reinforce British resistance to German threats,
although he was not confident of Chamberlain's resolve. Hull's
opposition to "going too far" seemed to kill a Treasury plan to
protect British and French gold, facilitate British arms purchases,
and impose trade sanctions on Germany.[90] But in a very secret
meeting with Lindsay on September 19, Roosevelt advanced those
ideas and others, warning Lindsay that "he would almost be
impeached" if what he said became known. A conference, which
he promised personally to attend if it were not held in Europe,

might postpone a crisis. But if war came he urged Britain to fight it "in a defensive manner," using blockade by land and sea. Lindsay noted that this was a direct extension of the "quarantine" and of FDR's several plans for imposing sanctions. As president, Roosevelt could declare such a blockade effective without having to consult Congress, and so the United States, wholly independently, would be able to cooperate with the British war effort. Further, Roosevelt urged that Britain not declare war so that he would not have to proclaim American neutrality, pointing out how that procedure had enabled him to avoid imposing the embargo on China. He also noted that the raw materials and unfinished parts for crucial munitions could legally be sent to Canada, where they could be assembled and sent across the Atlantic. He was careful to explain that London could not anticipate an American alliance, but short of that, he offered the fullest possible support.[91] In London, where things were hectic, his suggestions were virtually ignored. The Munich settlement made them all superfluous.

There had been only one real test of the ways in which Roosevelt expected a conference to be helpful: the Brussels conference of signatories of the Nine-Power Treaty in November 1937. At best, it demonstrated how failure might yield some benefits for Anglo-American relations. The conference was called to formulate a collective response to Japanese aggression, and closely followed Roosevelt's "quarantine" speech, with its implication of a readiness to act. Yet Brussels produced no plan to stop the war in Asia and so was an immense disappointment to most supporters of collective security. In the context of years of mistrust between the United States and Britain on Asian policy, however, and in the absence of any agreement between them for cooperation in the current crisis, the conference did have the positive attribute of unambiguously identifying Japan as the aggressor, and thus clarifying the identity of British and American interests. In part because of Brussels, Roosevelt felt confident enough to make some bold proposals for cooperative action when the situation in Asia grew worse.

From the beginning of his presidency, FDR had meant to "put Japan in the dock" for its aggression. His endorsement of MacDonald's disarmament plan anticipated that Japan would refuse to cooperate, and he embraced the 1932 Stimson Doctrine as the central American policy in the Pacific. The promises he and Davis made to support collective security in May 1933 were likewise based on the expectation that Tokyo would shun a nonaggression pact such as he proposed. And in determining American naval policy between 1933 and 1937, Roosevelt constantly strove to ostracize Japan and cooperate with Britain.[92]

These were difficult goals, for Britain's reaction to the Stimson Doctrine in 1932 left a bitterness in Washington to equal London's resentment over war debts and the failure of the economic conference. Whitehall disliked the hostility toward Japan it read in Roosevelt's policy, and it was not prepared to trust in American cooperation. When they contemplated simultaneous crises in Europe and Asia, Chamberlain, the military chiefs, and others longed to restore the Anglo-Japanese alliance. Their interest in closer relations with Tokyo so alarmed Washington that genuine Anglo-American cooperation seemed impossible.[93]

For Roosevelt the most congenial avenue for cooperation was naval policy. A treaty-mandated reconsideration of naval ratios by 1936 gave him three years to establish that London and Washington would not agree to Japanese demands for increased naval power, that they would maintain parity between them at a strength sufficient to counter Japan, and that it was Japan alone whose ambition doomed prospects for further naval disarmament. In addition, he hoped to use negotiations toward those objectives to develop a "united" policy that could "prevent war, or failing in that, to localize its area."[94]

FDR's decision to increase the U.S. Navy within current treaty limits in 1933 brought charges of "provocation" from both Tokyo and London, however. When he tried to demonstrate his friendly intentions by sending a squadron to visit the English fleet in its home ports, the British declined for fear of offending Japan. The president carried on, however, confidentially revealing his willingness to consider proposals for the closest cooperation in naval construction and even to arrange exchanges of naval personnel.[95] In discussions preliminary to the naval conference, his representatives insisted that Anglo-American parity and the rejection of Japanese demands were far more important than the official objective of reducing naval strengths. The British reaction was awkward and confusing. While it tried, for a time without telling the Americans, to reach an agreement with Tokyo, the national government declared that it needed some contractual guarantees from the United States before it could cooperate. It also insisted that Britain needed more ships in certain classes, increases over treaty limits that were likely to doom any new naval agreement in the Senate.

The State Department found London's position unacceptable on all counts, and the preliminary discussions seemed pointless until Roosevelt interceded to assure Lindsay that he would accept certain increases for the Royal Navy in consideration of its special needs. By such assurances, and helped greatly by the bellicosity of Japan, Roosevelt was primarily responsible for the Naval Treaty of 1936. Measured by the goal of naval reductions within quantitative limits, the treaty was a complete failure. Measured by FDR's intentions, it was a success. Japan's demands had been refused, and when Tokyo therefore declined to participate in the negotiations it branded itself as the destroyer of ratios, thus justifying the increases in the treaty. Britain had been dissuaded from a bilateral agreement with Japan, and had turned instead to the Americans, with whom it pledged itself in writing to maintain naval parity. London also understood that in spite of the treaty's new qualitative limits, Roosevelt would look sympathetically on any future requests for increases in specific classes.[96]

The treaty did not, of course, solve all of the problems of Anglo-American relations in the Pacific. Soon after the Rhineland coup the U.S. Navy proposed an exchange of intelligence data on a regular basis, but the Admiralty feared Japan might learn of the arrangement and said no. In spite of their eager pursuit of Treasury cooperation, Roosevelt and Morgenthau refused to join in a British financial mission to Asia in 1935 because they suspected London's intentions. Instead, the United States offered unilateral support to the Chinese currency.[97] The United States continued to decline "joint" action with Britain after July 1937, preferring a "parallel and identical" policy, which the Americans said would be less provocative but equally effective. Britons were impressed by the administration's standoffishness, but since Chamberlain had no interest in giving "joint" action the substance to make it effective, American doubts seem to have been prudent. While Eden wanted to discuss economic sanctions, Chamberlain and Hull, quite separately, opposed any option that might entail a risk.[98]

By declining to invoke the Neutrality Act Roosevelt had already demonstrated American sympathies. His "quarantine" speech went further by introducing his previously confidential ideas into the public arena. As usual, the British government was divided over the speech, Eden seeing in it hope for effective cooperation and Chamberlain suspecting that FDR meant to do something to imperil Anglo-Japanese relations or to saddle Britain with the blame for any failures. If Roosevelt intended the speech to revive British interest in cooperation, his subsequent complaint about the lack of "unselfish spine" in London is easy to understand.[99]

There was therefore no prospect of concrete action emerging from Brussels, from which FDR hoped for the reaffirmation of Anglo-American fidelity to principles, the ostracism of Japan, and possibly the creation of "some larger organisation of world Powers."[100] But the conference also gave him, through Norman Davis, a chance to explore ideas for future cooperation with Eden, and it may have been those discussions that prompted British suggestions for naval staff talks and a joint naval demonstration. Eden told Lindsay he had "good reason to believe [the United States] would seriously consider" such moves.[101] After the Japanese attacked the U.S.S. *Panay* and H.M.S. *Ladybird* in December 1937, Roosevelt considered those and more. He sent a naval officer to London to initiate ongoing discussions between the naval staffs, and, again relying on Morgenthau, he found authority to impose financial and economic sanctions on Japan. He also formulated plans for an Anglo-American blockade in the event of another outrage. London's cool response to all but the naval talks, in spite of Eden's eagerness to be supportive, ended considerations of any confrontational policy,[102] indicating that the earlier suggestions from Eden had not been vetted by the cabinet. After Munich, Roosevelt's encouragement of Britain to abandon appeasement was less oblique. While preventing a war was still his hope, and while keeping the United States out of war remained his purpose, helping Britain win a war that could not be avoided was the thrust of his proposals. Only a few days after the crisis ended he talked with a British friend to whom he gave messages for the leaders of the governments in Ottawa and London. With the Canadians, his suggestion led to air staff conversations aimed primarily at coordinating warplane production to increase volume and speed delivery. To Chamberlain he promised that Britain could rely on the "industrial resources of the American nation" for supplies, and that the Neutrality Act would not keep him from providing "partly finished basic materials" via Canada to insure air superiority over the dictator powers.[103] This was all consistent with what Roosevelt had promised Lindsay secretly in September, but the State Department either did not know of that promise or did not agree with it, for the ambassador learned that the department was planning to refuse licenses for shipments of strategic materials to Canada. By that time, however, the department's contradictions of FDR were almost meaningless. Whether on the question of shipments to Canada or providing direct financial aid to China, the president got his way, and in so doing obviously put the United States well ahead of London in its readiness to act.[104]

Roosevelt was frustrated by the pro-appeasement sentiment that continued in London in 1939, and especially by Chamberlain's dogged adherence to his policy.[105] He was at least equally perturbed by the readiness of some Britons to resign from the circle of great powers and let the United States assume the burden of protecting their interests—"this *morituri te salutamus* attitude," he was reported to have called it. If the English wanted his cooperation, he warned, they had to "make America believe . . . that they had enough backbone to retain their position by their own efforts and back the other guy on their own. . . . 'What the British need is a good stiff grog.' " He was prepared to stand aside if Britain "cringed like a coward." But "if only you British would give me a lead," he told another English friend, he would be able to bring the majority of Americans with him along the road to the closest and most urgent cooperation.[106]

That had been his thesis throughout the 1930s. His policy toward Great Britain was always based upon the need for a British posture that the American public would support. Members of the Foreign Office saw far sooner than others in their government that his proposals "were often less statements of policy than blueprints from which he would like to build." They appreciated his efforts to educate the American people about world affairs, and they knew that the record of British appeasement made his task incalculably more difficult.[107] It is impossible to know whether any of Roosevelt's ideas might actually have prevented the war by confronting the dictators early with effective collective measures supported by the United States. It is equally impossible to declare that none of them could have done that. It is true that the president's confidential overtures did not of themselves constitute an effective foreign policy, but it is also true that because of Roosevelt there was an alternative available to appeasement, and that thanks mostly to Chamberlain it was never fully explored.

NOTES

1. Thomas Jones, *A Diary with Letters, 1931–1950* (London: Oxford University Press, 1954), p. 30; Keith Feiling, *The Life of Neville Chamberlain* (London: Macmillan, 1946), p. 325.

2. A. J. P. Taylor, in *Origins of the Second World War* (New York: Atheneum, 1962), simply dismisses the United States as a factor in British policymaking. Less peremptory but equally definite is D. C. Watt, "The Breakdown of the European Security System 1930–1939," 14th International Conference of Historical Sciences (San Francisco, Calif., August 1975). Most scholars have sought to explain the assumed ineffectuality of American policy. Robert Dallek's *Franklin D. Roosevelt and American Foreign Policy, 1932–1945* (New

York: Oxford University Press, 1979), the most comprehensive treatment, attributes it to domestic problems and Washington's uncertainty about the nation's international goals. William L. Langer and S. Everett Gleason, *The Challenge to Isolation: The World Crisis of 1937–1940 and American Foreign Policy* (New York: Harper and Row, 1964), notes a shift to a more active policy late in the decade, as does David Reynolds in *The Creation of the Anglo-American Alliance, 1937–1941: A Study in Competitive Co-Operation* (Chapel Hill: University of North Carolina Press, 1982). His brief but perceptive discussion of the period before 1939 expands on Dallek to include Roosevelt's confusing management techniques and his tendency to toss out what seemed to be ill-conceived notions as additional factors. Reynolds's emphasis is on the issues that divided the United States and Britain until those issues were temporarily suppressed in 1939. These divisive issues are also the focus of C. A. MacDonald's *The United States, Britain and Appeasement, 1936–1939* (New York: St. Martin's Press, 1981), which concentrates on the economic competition between the two governments, a topic earlier explored by Lloyd C. Gardner in *Economic Aspects of New Deal Diplomacy* (Madison: University of Wisconsin Press, 1964) and Warren F. Kimball in "Lend-Lease and the Open Door: The Temptation of British Opulence, 1937–1942," *Political Science Quarterly* 86 (1971): 232–59. A provocative and more convicting explanation for the absence of any effective Anglo-American cooperation is implicit in Arnold Offner, *American Appeasement: United States Foreign Policy and Germany, 1933–1938* (New York: W. W. Norton, 1969), which sees the United States pursuing its own appeasement of the Third Reich based upon both selfishness and clumsiness.

    3. Reynolds, *Creation of the Anglo-American Alliance*, p. 18.

    4. N. Gordon Levin, Jr., *Woodrow Wilson and World Politics: American Responses to War and Revolution* (New York: Oxford University Press, 1968), p. 260.

    5. Dallek, *Roosevelt and American Foreign Policy*, p. 342.

    6. For the application of this principle to the idea of an "arsenal of democracy," see John Lewis Gaddis, *Strategies of Containment: A Critical Appraisal of Postwar American National Security Policy* (New York: Oxford University Press, 1982), pp. 6–7.

    7. See, e.g., Reynolds, *Creation of the Anglo-American Alliance*, pp. 34–36; Watt, "Breakdown of European Security System," p. 14.

    8. See, e.g., Osborne to Simon, August 27, 1933, FO371, 16612/A6330/252/45, Archives of the Foreign Office, Public Records Office, London (hereafter cited as PRO).

    9. Frank Freidel, *F.D.R.: Launching the New Deal* (Boston: Little, Brown, 1973), pp. 355–57.

    10. Watt, "Breakdown of European Security System," p. 14. The State Department's record in pursuit of changes in the international commercial

regime that would favor the United States is the basis for historical interpretations, such as MacDonald's in *The United States, Britain and Appeasement*,
based exclusively on the narrow ground of economic policy.
   11. John M. Blum, ed., *The Price of Vision: Diary of Henry A. Wallace,
1942–1946* (Boston: Houghton Mifflin, 1973), p. 271.
   12. Osborne to Simon, August 27, 1933, FO371, 16612/A6330/252/45,
PRO.
   13. Claudel to Paul Boncour, April 5, 1933, (France) Ministere des Affaires
Etrangeres, Commission de Publication des Documents Relatifs aux Origines
de la Guerre 1939–1945, *Documents Diplomatiques Francais 1932–1939* (hereafter cited as *Documents Diplomatiques*), 1 ser., vol. 3, p. 149.
   14. Cummings to Runciman, September 9, 1932, WR259, Runciman of
Doxford Papers, University of Newcastle-upon-Tyne; Lindsay to Simon, January 30, 1933, (Great Britain) Foreign Office, *Documents on British Foreign
Policy, 1919–1939*, E. L. Woodward et al., eds. (hereafter cited as *DBFP*),
2 ser., vol. 5, pp. 748–51.
   15. Committee on Imperial Defence (CID), "Imperial Defence Policy," June
1933, #1112-B, Cab 4/22, British Cabinet Papers, PRO; Lindsay to Simon,
January 30, 1933, *DBFP*, 2 ser., vol. 5, p. 769 ("legal side").
   16. Cummings to Runciman, September 9, 1932, WR259, Runciman Papers;
Claudel to Paul Boncour, April 5, 1933, *Documents Diplomatiques*, 1 ser., vol.
3, pp. 149, 153; Lindsay to Simon, February 21, 1933, *DBFP*, 2 ser., vol. 5, pp.
769–71.
   17. Lindsay to Simon, February 21, 1933, *DBFP*, 2 ser., vol. 5, pp. 769–71.
   18. Minutes on Lindsay to Simon, January 30, 1933, FO371,
16666/C853/1/62, PRO; minutes of Cabinet Committee on Debts, February 6,
1933, BDA(33) 1st meeting, Cab 27/548/73365, Cabinet Papers; Lothian to
House, February 13, 1933, E. M. House Papers, Yale University Library (with
permission of Yale University Library); Leith-Ross to Chamberlain, March 27,
1935, T175/79, Treasury Papers, PRO.
   19. Memorandum by Runciman, March 31, 1933, WR259, Runciman Papers, *DBFP*, 2 ser., vol. 5, p. 793n; Lindsay to Simon, May 22, 1933, pp. 810–11.
   20. Lindsay to Simon, May 22, 1933, T175/1815; file T188/74/73253;
Phillips to Chamberlain, June 6, 1933, T177/17, Treasury Papers; Lindsay to
Simon, June 4, 1933, *DBFP*, 2 ser., vol. 5, pp. 815–17, November 1, 1933,
pp. 852–53; Cabinet Conclusions, 66(33), November 29, 1933, Cabinet Papers.
   21. Simon to Lindsay, April 30, 1934, T188/75, Treasury Papers. Hull was
spared any specific mention, perhaps because he took pains to tell Lindsay that
FDR, but not he, had agreed to the act. (Lindsay to Simon, April 19, 1934,
DBFP, 2 ser., vol. 5, p. 910.
   22. Lindsay to Simon, May 6, 1934, *DBFP*, 2 ser., vol. 5, pp. 916–17
("astonishing"), May 16, 1934, p. 925; Leith-Ross to Lindsay, May 7, 1934,
T188/75, Treasury Papers ("helpful").

23. See, e.g., Lindsay to Eden, March 22, 1937, FO371, 20651/A2378/38/45, PRO.
24. Lindsay to Simon, May 18, 1934, *DBFP*, 2 ser., vol. 5, pp. 926–29.
25. Frederick Leith-Ross, *Money Talks: Fifty Years of International Finance* (London: Hutchinson, 1968), p. 179.
26. Lindsay to Simon, January 27, 1933, *DBFP*, 2 ser., vol. 5, p. 750.
27. Report of Committee on Economic Information, May 16, 1933, C.P. 131(33), Cab 24/241, Cabinet Papers.
28. Freidel, *F.D.R.: Launching the New Deal*, pp. 485–86.
29. D. C. Watt, *Too Serious a Business: European Armed Forces and the Approach to the Second World War* (Berkeley: University of California Press, 1975), pp. 112–13; Diary entry of July 24, 1933, Robert W. Bingham Papers, Manuscripts Division, Library of Congress (DLC); Earl of Derby to Wiley, n.d. (July 1933), President's Personal File (PPF) 675, Franklin D. Roosevelt (FDR) Papers, Franklin D. Roosevelt Library, Hyde Park, New York (FDRL).
30. Notes for use in cabinet by Chamberlain, n.d., T172/2081, Treasury Papers.
31. Vansittart to Lindsay, September 26, 1934 (draft), vol. 109, Baldwin of Bewley Papers, Cambridge University Library.
32. File T160/845/13640/1, passim., esp. Stamp to Hopkins, May 6, 1936, Treasury Papers; memorandum by Cochran, October 15, 1935, Henry J. Morgenthau Diaries, FDRL; Bingham to Hull, June 3, 1935, 841.515/348, Department of State, National Archives (hereafter cited as NA), Washington, D.C.; John M. Blum, *From the Morgenthau Diaries*, vol. 1 (Boston: Houghton Mifflin, 1959), p. 141.
33. Memorandum by Fisher, May 24, 1935; memorandum by Phillips, May 30, 1935; memorandum by Hopkins, June 6, 1935, T160/845/13640/1, Treasury Papers.
34. Fisher to Vansittart, June 22, 1935, FO371, 18770/A5684/3169/45; Hamilton to Vansittart, June 27, 1935, /A5826/3169/45; Lindsay to Eden, February 5, 1936, FO414/273/A1302/1293/45; April 2, 1936, /A3026/890/45, PRO; memorandum by Davis, August 8, 1935, 500.A15A5/459, NA; Lindsay to Vansittart, August 8, 1935; Lindsay to Eden, January 23, 1936, T160/750/14239/1, Treasury Papers.
35. Entries of May 18, 1936, June 1, 1936, September 18, 1936, October 9, 1936; memorandum by Phillips, June 23, 1936, Morgenthau Diaries; memorandum by Phillips, May 27, 1936, 841.5151/554, NA; Eden to Lindsay, May 28, 1936; memorandum by Bewley, July 23, 1936, T160/845/13640/2, Treasury Papers; Blum, *From the Morgenthau Diaries*, vol. 1, p. 228.
36. Cummings to Runciman, September 9, 1932, WR259, Runciman Papers; Lindsay to Simon, January 27, 1933, *DBFP*, 2 ser., vol. 5, p. 750.
37. Memorandum by Runciman, March 31, 1933; Simpson to Runciman, April 4, 1934, WR259, Runciman Papers.

38. Lindsay to Vansittart, April 11, 1935, FO371, 18770/A4010/3169/45; Hoare to Lindsay, October 15, 1935, 18771/A8863/3169/45, PRO; Vansittart to Fisher, May 3, 1935; memorandum by Ashton-Gwatkin, September 4, 1935, T160/750/14239/1, Treasury Papers.
39. Memorandum by Hull, January 22, 1936, 611.4131/141A, NA; memorandum by Eden, February 7, 1936, FO371, 19884/C883/4/18, PRO.
40. Lindsay to Eden, April 2, 1936, T160/750/14239/2, Treasury Papers.
41. Feis to Hull, May 20, 1936, Cordell Hull Papers, DLC; Atherton to Hull, June 27, 1936, 841.5151/558; Bingham to Hull, September 19, 1936, 740.0011 Mutual Guarantee (Locarno)/797; Hull to Bingham, September 3, 1936, 611.4131/182A; Millard to Hull, November 10, 1936, 811.00/542, NA; Eden to Lindsay, September 19, 1936; Troutbeck to Waley, October 8, 1936; Waley to Leith-Ross, October 10, 1936, T160/750/14239/2; Lindsay to Eden, November 17, 1936; November 23, 1936; minutes of interdepartmental Meeting on Trade Negotiations with U.S.A., December 3, 1936; Eden to Lindsay, December 15, 1936, T160/750/14239/3, Treasury Papers; Lindsay to Eden, November 9, 1936, FO371, 19835/A9110/1293/45, PRO; Davis to Moffat, July 29, 1936, Norman H. Davis Papers, DLC.
42. Dunn to Moffat, December 19, 1936, Jay Pierrepont Moffat Papers, Harvard University Library (with permission of Harvard University Library); Bingham to House, December 21, 1936, House Papers (with permission of Yale University Library). It is unclear whether Bingham intended to include Hull in this opinion. Hull's colleagues in the department harbored a certain hostility toward the ambassador, who they believed was less than wholeheartedly committed to the secretary's program.
43. Runciman to Baldwin, February 8, 1937, FO371, 20656/A1059/93/45, PRO.
44. Richard A. Harrison, "The Runciman Visit to Washington in January 1937: Presidential Diplomacy and the Non-Commercial Implications of Anglo-American Trade Negotiations," *Canadian Journal of History/Annales Canadiennes d'Histoire* 19 (August 1984): 217–39.
45. Davis to Hull, April 29, 1937, 740.00/154, Section I; Bingham to Hull, April 30, 1937, /155, NA.
46. Blum, *From the Morgenthau Diaries*, vol. 1, p. 524.
47. FDR to Phillips, May 17, 1937, in Elliott Roosevelt, ed., *F.D.R.: His Personal Letters, 1928–1945*, 2 vols. (New York, 1950) (hereafter cited as *Personal Letters*), vol. 1, p. 680.
48. Cummings to Runciman, September 9, 1932, WR259, Runciman Papers.
49. Lindsay to Simon, January 30, 1933, *DBFP*, 2 ser., vol. 5, p. 750. Claudel to Paul Boncour, April 5, 1933, *Documents Diplomatiques*, 1 ser., vol. III, p. 149; de Laboulaye to Paul Boncour, April 19, 1933, p. 246.
50. Gibson to Hull, March 8, 1933, U.S. Department of State, *Foreign Relations of the United States: Diplomatic Papers* (hereafter cited as *FRUS*),

1933, vol. 1, pp. 25–27; March 12, 1933, pp. 32–33; Hull to Gibson, March 10, 1933, pp. 29–30; Hull to Wilson, April 24, 1933, pp. 102–4 ("Monroe Doctrine"); Davis to Hull, April 25, 1933, pp. 106–7; May 19, 1933, pp. 154–58.
Entries of April 22, 24, 25, 28, May 4, 1933, Moffat Journals; Moffat to Wilson, May 9, 1933, May 16, 1933, Moffat Papers (with permission of Harvard University Library); Hull to Davis, April 28, 1933, 500.A15A4 General Committee/339, NA; Vansittart to Simon, April 25, 1933, FO800/288, PRO.
    51. Atherton to Hull, May 17, 1933, 500.A15A4/1867; May 18, 1933, /2007; Bingham to Hull, May 19, 1933, /1912, NA; Cabinet Conclusion 35(33)3, May 17, 1933, Cab 23/76, Cabinet Papers; Bingham to FDR, May 22, 1933, Edgar B. Nixon, ed., *Franklin D. Roosevelt and Foreign Affairs* (hereafter cited as *FDRFA*), 3 vols. (Cambridge, Mass.: Belknap Press of Harvard University Press, 1969), vol. 1, pp. 158–59. *The (London) Times*, May 23, 1933, p. 15; minutes by Smith, May 17, 1933, *DBFP*, 2 ser., vol. 5, pp. 248–50; memorandum by Leeper, May 29, 1933, pp. 282–83; memorandum by Reynolds, May 31, 1933, pp. 303–5.
    52. John W. Wheeler-Bennett, *The Pipe Dream of Peace: The Story of the Collapse of Disarmament* (New York: William Morrow, 1971), pp. 86–126, esp. 124; memorandum by Phillips, June 1, 1933, 811.113/317, NA.
    53. Address to the Woodrow Wilson Foundation, December 28, 1933, *Public Papers and Addresses of Franklin D. Roosevelt* (hereafter cited as *PPA*), vol. 2, p. 548; Sweetser to Drummond, January 13, 1934, Arthur Sweetser Papers, DLC.
    54. Atherton to Hull, January 2, 1934, *FRUS*, 1934, vol. 1, pp. 1–4; State Department to British Embassy, February 19, 1934, pp. 22–23; Hull to Davis, March 28, 1934, pp. 34–35; Davis to Hull, March 31, 1934, pp. 36–37; April 6, 1934, pp. 42–44; Report of Sub-Committee on Economic Pressure of CID Committee on Trade Questions in Time of War, October 30, 1933, #1118-B, Cab 4/22; Cabinet Memorandum, C.P. 68(34), March 9, 1934; C.P. 82(34), March 21, 1934, Cab 24/248, Cabinet Papers; minutes of February 1934, FO371, 18516/W1072/1/98; Delegation at Geneva to FO, May 28, 1934, /W52401/1/98; Selby to Sargent, June 5, 1934, Au/34/4. FO800/272, PRO; Davis to FDR, January 25, 1934, 711.00111/54; Davis to Hull, March 31, 1934, 500.A15A4/2460; Bingham to Hull, May 19, 1934, 793.94/6691, NA; FDR Press Conference, March 23, 1934, *FDRFA*, vol. 2, p. 30; Bingham to FDR, April 23, 1934, p. 79; Notes by Cecil, March 28, 1934, Add. Mss. 51080, Cecil of Chelwood Papers, Manuscripts Division, British Library; Entries of March 25, 1934 ("limited liabilities"), April 20, 1934, Diary of Neville Chamberlain, NC2/23a, Neville Chamberlain Papers, Birmingham University Library (with permission of Birmingham University Library); entry of March 27, 1934, Bingham Diary.
    55. Hull to Davis, April 2, 1934, *FRUS*, 1934, vol. 1, pp. 37–38; memorandum by Phillips, May 25, 1934, p. 70; Phillips to Moffat, October 22, 1934,

p. 170; Moffat to Phillips, October 23, 1934, pp. 170–72; memorandum by Moffat, July 14, 1934, 711.41/275, NA; memorandum by Davis, April 28, 1934, Davis Papers.

56. Atherton to Hull, January 31, 1935, 500.C114/1592, NA; Atherton to Bingham, February 5, 1935, Bingham Papers; Lindsay to Simon, February 13, 1935, FO115/3407/88, PRO.

57. Entry of March 18, 1935, Morgenthau Diaries; memorandum by Davis, March 19, 1935, Davis papers; FDR to House, April 10, 1935, *FDRFA*, vol. II, pp. 488–89; Johnson to Hull, April 2, 1935, 741.62/73; Atherton to Hull, April 17, 1935, 852.20/940; April 25, 1935, 862.20/980; Bingham to Hull, April 29, 1935, 841.002/139; Memorandum by Field, June 8, 1935, 862.34/146, NA; Bingham to House, April 24, 1935, House Papers (with permission of Yale University Library). Report of Sub-Committee on Economic Pressure of CID Advisory Committee on Trade Questions in Time of War, #1175, June 3, 1935, Cab 4/23; minutes of CID #270, July 11, 1935, Cab 2/6, Cabinet Papers; Atherton to Hull, March 19, 1935, *FRUS, 1935*, vol. II, pp. 304–5; Emmet to Hull, April 2, 1935, vol. 2, pp. 216–17.

58. FDR to Bingham, July 11, 1935, *FDRFA*, vol. 2, p. 554. FDR to Bullitt, April 21, 1935, *Personal Letters*, vol. 1, p. 476 ("continental damn").

59. FDR Press Conference, August 28, 1935, *FDRFA*, vol. 2, p. 623.

60. Memorandum by American Department, September 20, 1935, FO371, 19139/J5429/1/1; minutes on Memorandum by Malkin, November 20, 1935, 18772/A10408/3483/45; Lindsay to Hoare, November 29, 1935, 19217/J8665/5499/1; MacDonald to Hoare, November 25, 1935, FO800/295, PRO; Seidel to Teagle, November 29, 1935; Teagle to Seidel, December 2, 1935; Ferguson to Chamberlain, November 29, 1935, T172/1838, Treasury Papers; Cabinet Conclusion 43(35)1, September 24, 1935; 45(35)1 & 6, October 9, 1935, 50(35)2, December 2, 1935, Cab 23/82, Cabinet Papers; Dawson to Lewis, October 8, 1935, Wilmott Lewis Papers; Barrington-Ward to Kennedy, January 10, 1936, R. G. Barrington-Ward Papers, Archives of *The Times*, London; Straus to Hull, November 8, 1935, 711.00111 Armament Control/421, NA; Feiling, *Chamberlain*, p. 272; Dearing to FDR, December 2, 1935, *FDRFA*, vol 3, p. 106. Anthony Eden, *Facing the Dictators* (Boston: Houghton Mifflin, 1962), p. 329.

61. Armstrong to Davis, December 13, 1935, Davis Papers. Notes by Ashton-Gwatkin, December 11, 1935, FO371, 19220/J9234/5499/1; Lindsay to Hoare, December 13, 1935, /J9747/5499/1; 19826/A1517/103/45; memorandum by Troutbeck, May 5, 1936, FO371, 20178/J4036/136/1, PRO; Harold L. Ickes, *The Secret Diary of Harold Ickes*, 3 vols. (New York: Simon and Schuster, 1953–54), vol. I, p. 484.

62. Entry of December 16, 1935, NC2/23a, Chamberlain Diary (with permission of Birmingham University Library); Cabinet Conclusion 54(35)3, December 11, 1935, Cab 23/82; Report of Sub-Committee on Economic Pres-

sure, CID Advisory Committee on Trade Questions in Time of War, #1188-B, September 18, 1935, Cab 4/23, Cabinet Papers; unsigned to Rowe-Dutton, September 4, 1935; memorandum by Phillips, September 5, 1935, T160/621/F14299/3, Treasury Papers; notes by Sweetser, April 4, 1938, Sweetser Papers.

63. Report of CID Advisory Committee on Trade Questions in Time of War, #1292-B, December 22, 1936, Cab 4/25, Cabinet Papers; Jones, *Diary with Letters*, p. 191.

64. FDR to Dodd, March 16, 1936, *Personal Letters*, vol. 1, p. 571; FDR to Biddle, April 15, 1936, p. 576; FDR to Morgenthau, May 22, 1936, *FDRFA*, vol. 3, p. 309. See, e.g., Willert to Craigie, April 9, 1936, and minutes, FO371, 19828/A3150/170/45, PRO ("jejune").

65. *New York Times*, August 26, 1936, p. 1; Lansbury to FDR, May 26, 1936, *FDRFA*, vol. 3, pp. 312–13; Woolley to FDR, April 10, 1936, p. 373; FDR to Dodd, August 5, 1936, *Personal Letters*, vol. 1, p. 606.

66. Steed to House, March 9, 1933, House Papers (with permission of Yale University Library); FDR to House, April 5, 1933, *Personal Letters*, vol. 1, p. 305.

67. Sweetser to FDR, January 30, 1937, PPF 506, FDR Papers; Memorandum by Sweetser, April 4, 1938, Sweetser Papers.

68. See, e.g., Jones to Baldwin, July 8, 1934, Baldwin Papers; Harding to Vansittart, January 16, 1934; Craigie to Lindsay, January 30, 1934, FO371, 17592/A566/566/45; Wrench to Vansittart, January 3, 1935, 18760/A531/531/45, PRO.

69. Memorandum by Sweetser, April 4, 1938, Sweetser Papers.

70. Bingham to Hull, September 19, 1936, 740.0011 Mutual Guarantee (Locarno)/797, NA.

71. Janet Adam Smith, *John Buchan* (London: Oxford University Press, 1965), p. 444; memorandum by M. MacDonald, September 21, 1936, FO371, 20476/W11944/79/98; Phipps to Eden, November 9, 1936, 19827/A8860/103/45, PRO. It is noteworthy that FDR used Dodd, for whom State Department professionals had no affection. (Moffat to Davis, October 7, 1936, Davis Papers.)

72. Eden minutes on Phipps to Eden, November 9, 1936; Vansittart to Lindsay, November 17, 1936, FO371, 19827/A8860/103/45, PRO.

73. See Richard A. Harrison, "Testing the Water: A Secret Probe toward Anglo-American Military Co-operation in 1936," *International History Review* 7, no. 2 (May 1985): 214–34; minutes of CID #283, October 29, 1936, Cab 2/6, Cabinet Papers; memorandum by Moore and Woodring, November 11, 1936, President's Secretary's File (PSF) 14, Confidential File (CF), War Department, FDR Papers. See file 300-T-78, Box 318; Dennys to Lee, November 30, 1936, Box 2561A, MID 9771-249/150, General Staff, Military Intelligence Division, War Department, National Archives; Ian Colvin, *The Chamberlain Cabinet:*

How the Meetings in 10 Downing Street, 1937–1939, led to the Second World War (London, 1971), pp. 27–29.

74. FDR to Dodd, January 9, 1937, *Personal Letters*, vol. 1, p. 649; McK. King to FDR, March 6, 1937, pp. 664–68. Gerard to FDR, January 29, 1937; March 17, 1937, PPF 977; memorandum by Dunn, February 27, 1937, PSF: Canada, 1933–1937, FDR Papers; Smith, *Buchan*, pp. 444–45, 473–75; Lindsay to Vansittart, March 8, 1937, FO371, 20670/A2082/2082/45; memorandum by Eden, March 20, 1937, 20651/A2197/38/45, PRO; memorandum by Davis, March 19, 1937, Davis Papers.

75. Entry of February 6, 1937, Morgenthau Diaries; Blum, *From the Morgenthau Diaries*, vol. 1, pp. 458–59; Eden, *Facing the Dictators*, p. 597; Memorandum by Bewley, February 23, 1937, T160/692/F15213, Treasury Papers.

76. John Harvey, ed., *The Diplomatic Diaries of Oliver Harvey, 1937–1940* (London: Collins, 1970), p. 17; minutes of CID #288, February 11, 1937, Cab 2/6, Cabinet Papers; Eden to Chamberlain, March 5, 1937; March 13, 1937 and minutes; Chamberlain to Eden, March 11, 1937, March 15, 1937; memorandum by Bewley, March 27, 1937, T160/692/F15213, Treasury Papers; Chamberlain to Morgenthau, March 26, 1937, 740.00/184, NA; Blum, *From the Morgenthau Diaries*, vol. 1, pp. 465–66.

77. Memorandum by Vansittart, December 16, 1936 and minutes, FO371, 19787/A9996/9996/51; Lindsay to Eden, December 22, 1936, /A0286/718/51; Runciman to Baldwin, February 8, 1937, FO371, 20656/A1059/93/4, PRO.

78. *Congressional Record*, vol. 81, part II, pp. 1683, 1778, 1782; Minutes by Fitzmaurice, March 23, 1937, FO371, 20666/A2721/448/45; Lindsay to Eden, April 30, 1937, /A3191/448/45; FO to Admiralty, April 9, 1937, FO414, 274/A1895/448/45, PRO.

79. FDR Press Conference, April 20, 1937, FDRL.

80. Davis to Bingham, June 10, 1937; Davis to Chamberlain, June 10, 1937; Chamberlain to Davis, July 8, 1937, Davis papers; memorandum by Eden, May 4, 5, 1937, FO371, 20660/A3417/228/45; June 17, 1937, /A4370/228/45; Lindsay to Eden, May 24, 1937, FO115/3414/1566, PRO; Eden to Chamberlain, June 17, 1937; FO to Prime Minister's Office, July 1, 1937 and minutes, PREM 1/261, Prime Minister's Papers; Bingham to Hull, June 10, 1937, 033.4111/338, NA.

81. FDR to Hull, July 7, 1937, Hull Papers.

82. Eden, *Facing the Dictators*, pp. 509–10, 514; memorandum by Moffat, August 31, 1937, 741.65/414; Biddle to Hull, July 30, 1937, /387, NA; Eden to Chamberlain, September 9, 1937, PREM 1/210, Prime Minister's Papers.

83. Hull Statement, July 16, 1937, *FRUS*, 1937, vol. 1, pp. 699–700; minutes on Eden to Lindsay, July 17, 1937, FO371, 20666/A5257/448/45 ("waste of time"), PRO; Ickes, *Secret Diary*, vol. 2, p. 213 ("take the ball").

84. Welles to FDR, October 6, 1937, *FRUS*, 1937, vol. 1, pp. 665–66; October 26, 1937, pp. 667–70; Sumner Welles, *Seven Decisions that Shaped*

History (New York: Harper and Brothers, 1950), pp. 22–23; Cordell Hull, *The Memoirs of Cordell Hull*, 2 vols. (New York: Macmillan, 1948), vol. 1, pp. 547–49. Welles seems to have taken the possibility of some concrete achievement by a conference more seriously than Roosevelt, whose more modest expectation that such a meeting would lead to closer Anglo-American cooperation in the future was also more realistic.

85. Notes by Cecil, November 13–15, 1937; Cecil to Vansittart, November 12, 1937, Add. Mss. 51178, Cecil of Chelwood Papers.

86. See Harvey, ed., *Diplomatic Diaries*, pp. 56, 58, 61; Johnson to Hull, November 16, 1937, 741.62/198, NA; Eden to Chamberlain, November 3, 1937, PREM 1/210, Prime Minister's Papers; Colvin, *Chamberlain Cabinet*, pp. 64–81.

87. FDR to McK. King, December 21, 1937; FDR to Welles, December 22, 1937; Armour to Welles, January 8, 1938, PSF Canada, 1933–1937; Welles to FDR, January 10, 1938; January 14, 1938, PSF State Department: Welles, FDR Papers; FDR to Taylor, December 28, 1937, *PPA*, vol. 6, pp. 554–55; David Dilks, ed., *Diaries of Sir Alexander Cadogan, 1938–1945* (New York: Putnam, 1971), pp. 32–33.

88. The record of FDR's proposal and the evolution of the British response is in file PREM 1/259, Prime Minister's Papers and in file FO371, 21526/A2127/64/45, PRO.

89. Minutes of Foreign Policy of Cabinet, F.P.(36)21, January 24, 1938, Cab 27/623, Cabinet Papers; Harvey, ed., *Diplomatic Diaries*, pp. 80, 84, 148 ("so rotten"). Halifax to Lindsay, March 11, 1938, FO371, 21526/A2127/64/45, PRO.

90. Entry of September 1, 1938, Morgenthau Diaries; Ickes, *Secret Diary*, vol. 2, p. 468; Blum, *From the Morgenthau Diaries*, vol. 1, pp. 514–19.

91. Lindsay to Halifax, September 19, 1938, FO371, 21527/A7504/64/45, PRO. FDR was thinking enough of calling a conference that he also mentioned it to a French visitor. See Nancy Harvison Hooker, ed., *The Moffat Papers: Selections from the Diplomatic Journals of Jay Pierrepont Moffat, 1919–1943* (Cambridge, Mass.: Harvard University Press, 1956), pp. 206–7; Ickes, *Secret Diary*, vol. 2, p. 474.

92. Freidel, *F.D.R.: Launching the New Deal*, pp. 120–21, 455–56; Long to FDR, July 17, 1933, *FDRFA*, vol. 1, p. 318.

93. Lindsay to Simon, January 21, 1932, *DBFP*, 2 ser., vol. 9, pp. 158–60; Wm. Roger Louis, *British Strategy in the Far East, 1919–1939* (Oxford: Clarendon Press, 1971), pp. 188–89; Brian Bond, *British Military Policy between the Two World Wars* (Oxford: Clarendon Press, 1980), p. 195; Bradford A. Lee, *Britain and the Sino-Japanese War, 1937–1939: A Study in the Dilemmas of British Decline* (Stanford, Calif.: Stanford University Press, 1973), pp. 7–8; CID Memorandum #1111, May 27, 1933, Cab 4/22; Report of Advisory Committee on Trade Questions in Time of War, #1126-B, December 20,

1933; CID Report #1144-B, June 1934, Cab 4/23; Cabinet Conclusion 57(33), October 26, 1933, Cab 23/77; 9(34)13, March 14, 1934, Cab 23/78; Cabinet Memorandum C.P. 80(34), March 16, 1934, Cab 24/248, Cabinet Papers; minute by Vansittart, December 15, 1933, FO371, 16612/A9235/252/45; Lindsay to Simon, January 3, 1934, FO115/3405/76/1, PRO; entry of March 25, 1934, NC2/23a, Chamberlain Diary (with permission of Birmingham University Library); entry of March 2, 1934, Bingham Diary; Hornbeck to Phillips, October 31, 1933, Hornbeck Papers.

94. Entry of February 20, 1934, Bingham Diary.

95. Freidel, *F.D.R.: Launching the New Deal*, p. 457; Cabinet Conclusions 50(33), September 5, 1933, Cab 23/77, Cabinet Papers; Simon to Osborne, September 6, 1933, FO371, 17366/W10191/40/98; Barnes to Vansittart, January 24, 1933 and minutes, 17593/A785/45, PRO; Davis to Hull, September 6, 1933, *FRUS*, 1933, vol. 1, pp. 212–14; September 18, 1933, pp. 214–17; Osborne to Simon, September 14, 1933, *DBFP*, 2 ser., vol. 5, pp. 589–90; Moffat to Davis, September 25, 1933, 811.34/539, NA; Lewis to Dawson, February 21, 1934, Lewis Papers.

96. Memorandum by Davis, April 28, 1934; June 20, 1934; Bingham to Davis, May 23, 1934; Moffat to Davis, May 28, 1934; July 2, 1934, Davis Papers; Bingham to Davis, May 2, 1934; Moffat to Hull, May 3, 1934, 500.A15A5/42; Davis to Hull, June 21, 1934, /104; Davis to FDR, June 28, 1934, /118, NA; Hull to Davis, May 24, 1934, *FRUS*, 1934, vol. 1, pp. 238–39; November 22, 1934, pp. 364–65; memorandum by Moffat, September 11, 1934, p. 305; Davis to Hull, October 27, 1934, p. 317; FDR to Hull, November 14, 1934, pp. 333–34; December 7, 1934, pp. 390–91; memorandum by Field, September 17, 1935, *FRUS*, 1935, vol. 1, pp. 112–13; FDR to Davis, November 9, 1934, *FDRFA*, vol. 1, p. 263; Cabinet Conclusion 32(34)5, September 25, 1934, Cab 23/79; memorandum by CID, #1283-B, December 22, 1936, Cab 4/25, Cabinet Papers; memorandum by Craigie, July 2, 1934; Jones to Baldwin, July 8, 1934; Fisher to Chatfield, July 11, 1934, Baldwin Papers; memorandum by Chamberlain, September 1934, NC8/19/1, Chamberlain Papers; entry of October 9, 1934, NC2/23a, Chamberlain Diary (with permission of Birmingham University Library).

97. Admiralty to FO, March 25, 1936, FO371, 19836/A2494/2494/45; memorandum by Gore-Booth, March 30, 1936, /A3291/2494/45, PRO; entry of July 9, 1935, Morgenthau Diaries; Peck to Hull, October 4, 1935, Correspondence: State Department, Morgenthau Papers; Blum, *From the Morgenthau Diaries*, vol. 1, pp. 227–28.

98. Cabinet Conclusion 32(37)5, July 28, 1937, Cab 23/89, Cabinet Papers; memorandum by Far East Division, August 30, 1937; Eden to Mallet, September 30, 1937, PREM 1/314, Prime Minister's Papers; Eden to Lindsay, September 30, 1937; Admiralty to FO, October 4, 1937, T160/1034/F15255/1,

Treasury Papers; Hooker, ed., *Moffat Papers*, p. 153; Harvey, ed., *Diplomatic Diaries*, pp. 48–49.

99. Cabinet Conclusion 36(37)5, October 6, 1937; 37(37)5m, October 13, 1937, Cab 23/89, Cabinet Papers; draft of Eden to Mallet, Vansittart to Chamberlain, October 8, 1937, PREM 1/314, Prime Minister's Papers; FDR to Murray, October 7, 1937, *Personal Letters*, vol. 1, p. 716 ("unselfish spine").

100. Eden to Lindsay, October 28, 1937, FO371, 20663/A7748/228/45, PRO.

101. Eden to Lindsay, November 27, 1937; December 6, 1937 ("good reason"); Lindsay to Eden, November 29, 1937; December 1, 1937, T160/693/F15255/01, Treasury Papers.

102. Lindsay to Eden, December 14, 1937; memorandum by Simon, December 18, 1937; Simon to Chamberlain, December 18, 1937, T160/693/F15255/01, Treasury Papers; Cabinet Conclusion 48(37)5, December 22, 1937, Cab 23/90, Cabinet Papers; Lindsay to Eden, December 15, 1937 and minutes, FO371, 20961/F11201/9/10; Blum, *From the Morgenthau Diaries*, vol. 1, pp. 486–93; Ickes, *Secret Diary*, vol. 2, pp. 274–75, 277; Harvey, ed., *Diplomatic Diaries*, pp. 64–65; Eden, *Facing the Dictators*, p. 620.

103. Notes by Murray, October 23, 1938; December 14, 1938; Murray to Wood, December 15, 1938; December 21, 1938, Arthur Murray Papers 8809, Murray of Elibank Papers, National Library of Scotland; Murray to FDR, December 15, 1938, PSF 53, FDR Papers.

104. Lindsay to Balfour, November 1, 1938, FO371, 21527/A8474/64/45, PRO; entry of December 18, 1938, manuscript Diary of Harold L. Ickes, DLC; Harvey, ed., *Diplomatic Diaries*, pp. 230–31; Cabinet Conclusion 1(39)3, January 18, 1939; 2(39)3, February 1, 1939, Cab 23/97, Cabinet Papers.

105. Kennedy to Hull, February 17, 1939, 740.00/588, NA.

106. Vyvyan to Strang, March 4, 1939, FO371, 22827/A1143/1143/45, PRO ("stiff grog"); Ickes, *Secret Diary*, vol. 2, p. 571 ("like a coward"); Harvey, ed., *Diplomatic Diaries*, p. 259; Memorandum by Willert, March 25–26, 1939, FP(36)80, Cab 27/627/73365, Cabinet Papers ("give me a lead").

107. Minutes by Montagu-Douglas-Scott on Lindsay to Halifax, November 10, 1938, FO371, 21527/A8441/64/45/PRO.

Selected Bibliography

PRIMARY SOURCES

Public Documents and Government Publications

Berle, Beatrice B., and Travis Beal Jacobs, eds. *Navigating the Rapids 1918–1971: From the Papers of Adolf A. Berle.* New York: Harcourt Brace Jovanovich, 1973.

Blum, John Morton, ed. *From the Morgenthau Diaries: Years of Crisis, 1928–1938.* Boston: Houghton Mifflin, 1959.

Bullitt, Orville H., ed. *For the President, Personal and Secret: Correspondence Between Franklin D. Roosevelt and William C. Bullitt.* Boston: Houghton Mifflin, 1972.

Dodd, William E., and Martha Dodd. *Ambassador Dodd's Diary, 1933–1938.* New York: Harcourt, Brace and Company, 1941.

Hooker, Nancy Harvison. *The Moffat Papers: Selections from the Diplomatic Journals of Jay Pierrepont Moffat 1919–1943.* Cambridge, Mass.: Harvard University Press, 1956.

Ickes, Harold. *The Secret Diary of Harold Ickes,* 3 vols. New York: Simon and Schuster, 1953–1954.

Lary, Hal B., et al. *The United States in the World Economy.* Department of Commerce Economic Series No. 23. Washington, D.C.: Government Printing Office, 1943.

Nixon, Edgar B. *Franklin D. Roosevelt and Foreign Affairs,* 3 vols. Cambridge, Mass.: Belknap Press of Harvard University Press, 1969.

Roosevelt, Elliot, ed. *F.D.R.: His Personal Letters, 1928–1945,* 2 vols. New York: Duell, Sloan and Pearce, 1950.

Roosevelt, Franklin D. *Complete Presidential Press Conferences of Franklin D. Roosevelt, 1933–1945*, 12 vols. New York: DeCapo Press, 1972.

Rosenman, Samuel, ed. *The Public Papers and Addresses of Franklin D. Roosevelt*, 13 vols. New York: Random House, 1938–1950.

Schewe, Donald B., ed. *Franklin D. Roosevelt and Foreign Affairs*, 11 vols. New York: Garland Press, 1979.

U.S. Department of Commerce. *Foreign Commerce and Navigation of the United States, 1921–1940*. Washington, D.C.: Government Printing Office, 1922–1942.

U.S. Department of State. *Foreign Relations of the United States, 1921–1940*. Washington, D.C.: Government Printing Office, 1936–1957.

———. *Documents on German Foreign Policy, 1918–1941*. Washington, D.C.: Government Printing Office, 1957–1966.

———. *Peace and War: United States Foreign Policy, 1931–1941*. Washington, D.C.: Government Printing Office, 1943.

Autobiographies and Memoirs

Bowers, Claude. *My Mission to Spain: Watching the Rehearsal for World War II*. New York: Simon and Schuster, 1954.

Hoover, Herbert. *Memoirs, The Cabinet and the Presidency*, volume II. New York: Macmillan, 1952.

Hull, Cordell. *The Memoirs of Cordell Hull*, 2 vols. New York: Macmillan, 1948.

Kennan, George F. *Memoirs, 1925–1950*. Boston: Little, Brown, 1967.

Krock, Arthur. *Memoirs: Sixty Years on the Firing Line*. New York: Popular Library, 1968.

Mussolini, Benito. *My Autobiography*. New York: C. Scribner's, 1928.

Phillips, William. *Ventures in Diplomacy*. Boston: Beacon Press, 1952.

Simon, Viscount. *Retrospect: The Memoirs of the Rt. Hon. Viscount Simon*. London: Hutchinson, 1952.

Stimson, Henry L. and McGeorge Bundy. *On Active Service in Peace and War*. New York: Harper and Brothers, 1947.

Welles, Sumner. *The Time for Decision*. New York: Harper and Brothers, 1944.

———. *Seven Decisions That Shaped History*. New York: Harper and Brothers, 1951.

Wilson, Hugh R. *Diplomat Between Wars*. New York: Longmans, Green and Co., 1941.

SECONDARY SOURCES

Articles

Allen, William R. "International Trade Philosophy of Cordell Hull, 1907–1933." *American Economic Review* 43 (March 1953): 101–16.
————. "Cordell Hull and the Defense of Trade Agreements Program, 1934–1940." In Alexander De Conde, ed., *Isolation and Security: Ideas and Interests in Twentieth Century American Foreign Policy*. Durham, N.C.: Duke University Press, 1957.
Askew, William C. "The Secret Agreement Between France and Italy on Ethiopia, January 1935." *Journal of Modern History* 25 (March 1953): 47–48.
Borg, Dorothy. "Notes on Roosevelt's Quarantine Speech." *Political Science Quarterly* 72 (September 1957): 405–33.
Braddick, Henderson B. "A New Look at American Policy during the Italo-Ethiopian Crisis, 1935–1936." *Journal of Modern History* 34 (March 1962): 64–73.
Cole, Wayne S. "American Entry into World War II: A Historiographical Appraisal." *Mississippi Valley Historical Review* 43 (March 1957): 595–617.
————. "Senator Key Pittman and American Neutrality Policies, 1933–1940." *Mississippi Valley Historical Review* 44 (March 1960): 644–62.
Craig, Gordon A. "The German Foreign Office from Neurath to Ribbentrop." In Craig and Gilbert, eds., *The Diplomats*. New York: Atheneum, 1963.
————. "Totalitarian Approaches to Diplomatic Negotiation." In A. O. Sarkissian, ed., *Studies in Diplomatic History and Historiography in Honour of G. P. Gooch, C.H.* London: Longmans, 1961.
Dallek, Robert. "Beyond Tradition: The Diplomatic Careers of William E. Dodd and George S. Messersmith, 1933–1938." *South Atlantic Quarterly* 66 (Spring 1977): 233–44.
Divine, Robert A. "Franklin D. Roosevelt and Collective Security, 1933." *Mississippi Valley Historical Review* 48 (June 1961): 42–59.
Doenecke, Justus D. "Beyond Polemics: An Historiographic Re-Appraisal of American Entry into World War II." *History Teacher* 12, no. 2 (1979): 217–51.
Drummond, Donald F. "Cordell Hull." In Graebner, ed., *An Uncertain Tradition*. New York: McGraw Hill, 1961.
Edwards, P. G. "The Foreign Office and Fascism 1924–1929." *Journal of Contemporary History* 5 (1970): 153–61.
Ford, Franklin L. "Three Observers in Berlin: Rumbold, Dodd, and Francois-Poncet." In Craig and Gilbert, eds., *The Diplomats*. New York: Atheneum, 1963.

Friedlander, Robert A. "New Light on the Anglo-American Reaction to the Ethiopian War, 1935–1936." *Mid-America* 45 (1963): 115–25.

Haight, Jr., John McV. "France, the United States, and the Munich Conference." *Journal of Modern History* 32 (December 1960): 340–58.

————. "Roosevelt and the Aftermath of the Quarantine Speech," *Review of Politics* 24 (April 1962): 233–59.

Harrison, Richard A. "A Presidential Demarche: Franklin D. Roosevelt's Personal Diplomacy and Great Britain, 1936–1937." *Diplomatic History* 5, no. 2 (Summer 1981): 245–72.

————. "The Runciman Visit to Washington in January 1937: Presidential Diplomacy and the Non-Commercial Implications of Anglo-American Trade Negotiations." *Canadian Journal of History/Annales Canadiennes d'Histoire* 19 (August 1984): 217–39.

————. "Testing the Water: A Secret Probe toward Anglo-American Military Co-operation in 1936." *International History Review* 7, no. 2 (May 1985): 214–34.

Hilton, Stanley E. "The Welles Mission to Europe, February–March 1940: Illusion or Realism." *Journal of American History* 58 (June 1971): 93–120.

Jacobs, Travis Beal. "Roosevelt's Quarantine Speech." *The Historian* 24 (August 1962): 483–502.

Jonas, Manfred. "Prophet Without Honor: Hans Heinrich Dieckhoff's Reports from Washington." *Mid-America* 47 (July 1965): 222–33.

Kaufmann, William W. "Two American Ambassadors: Bullitt and Kennedy." In Craig and Gilbert, eds., *The Diplomats*. New York: Atheneum, 1963.

Kimball, Warren F. "Dieckhoff and America: A German's View of German-American Relations, 1937–1941." *The Historian* 27 (February 1965): 218–43.

————. "Lend-Lease and the Open Door: The Temptation of British Opulence, 1937–1948." *Political Science Quarterly* 86 (1971): 232–59.

Kolko, Gabriel. "American Business and Germany, 1930–1941." *Western Political Quarterly* 15 (December 1962): 713–28.

Lerner, Max. "Behind Hull's Embargo." *The Nation* (28 May 1938): 607–10.

Little, Douglas. "Twenty Years of Turmoil: ITT, The State Department, and Spain, 1924–1944." *Business History Review* (Winter 1979): 449–72.

————. "Claude Bowers and His Mission to Spain." In K. Paul Jones, ed., *U.S. Diplomats in Europe, 1919–1941*. Santa Barbara, Calif.: ABC-Clio, 1981.

MacDonald, C. A. "Economic Appeasement and the German 'Moderates' 1937–1939." *Past and Present* 56 (August 1972): 105–35.

Marks III, Frederick W. "Six Between Roosevelt and Hitler: America's Role in the Appeasement of Nazi Germany." *Historical Journal* (December 1985): 969–82.

Migone, Gian G. "La Stabilizzazione della lira: La finanza americana e Mussolini." *Rivista di storia contemporanea* 2, no. 2 (April 1973): 145–85.

———. "Le origini dell'egomonia americana in Europa." *Rivista di storia contemporanea* 3, no. 4 (October 1974): 433–59.

Moss, Kenneth. "George S. Messersmith: An American Diplomat and Nazi Germany." *Delaware History* 17 (Fall and Winter 1977): 236–49.

———. "The United States, the Open Door, and Nazi Germany: 1933–1938." *South Atlantic Quarterly* 78 (Autumn 1979): 489–506.

Nichols, Jeannette P. "Roosevelt's Monetary Diplomacy in 1933." *American Historical Review* 56 (January 1951): 295–317.

Norman, John. "Influence of Pro-Fascist Propaganda on American Neutrality, 1935–1936." In Dwight E. Lee and George E. McReynolds, eds., *Essays in History and International Relations in Honor of George Hubbard Blakeslee*. Worcester, Mass.: Clark University, 1949.

Offner, Arnold A. "William E. Dodd: Romantic Historian and Diplomatic Cassandra." *The Historian* 24 (August 1962): 451–69.

———. "Appeasement Revisited: The United States, Great Britain, and Germany, 1933–1940." *Journal of American History* 64 (September 1977): 363–93.

———. "The United States and National Socialist Germany." In Wolfgang J. Mommsen and Lothar Kettenacker, eds., *Fascist Challenge and the Policy of Appeasement*. London: George Allen & Unwin, 1983.

Parker, R. A. C. "Great Britain, France, and the Ethiopian Crisis, 1935–1936." *English Historical Review* 89, no. 351 (1971): 293–332.

Remak, Joachim. "'Friends of the New Germany': The Bund and German-American Relations." *Journal of Modern History* 29 (March 1957).

———. "Two German Views of the United States: Hitler and His Diplomats." *World Affairs Quarterly* 28 (April 1957): 38–41.

Richardson, Charles O. "The Rome Accords of January 1935 and the Coming of the Italian-Ethiopian War." *Historian* 41, no. 1 (1978): 41–58.

Robertson, James C. "The Hoare-Laval Plan," *Journal of Contemporary History* 10, no. 3 (1975): 433–64.

Rock, William. "British Appeasement (1930's); A Need for Revision?" *The South Atlantic Quarterly* 78, no. 3 (Summer 1979): 290–301.

Schatz, Arthur W. "The Anglo-American Trade Agreement and Cordell Hull's Search for Peace, 1936–1938." *Journal of American History* 62 (June 1970): 85–103.

Schmitt, Bernadotte E. "Munich." *Journal of Modern History* 25 (June 1953): 166–80.

Schröder, Hans-Jurgen. "The Ambiguities of Appeasement: Great Britain, the United States and Germany, 1937–9." In Wolfgang J. Mommsen and Lothar Kettenacker, eds., *The Fascist Challenge and the Policy of Appeasement*. London: George Allen & Unwin, 1983.

Shorrock, William I. "France and the Rise of Fascism in Italy, 1919–23."
    Journal of Contemporary History 10 (1975): 591–610.
————. "The Jouvenel Mission to Rome and the Origins of the Laval-Mussolini
    Accords, 1933–1935." *The Historian* 45 (November 1982): 20–30.
Smith, Robert Freeman. "American Foreign Relations, 1920–1942." In Barton
    J. Bernstein, ed., *Towards A New Past: Dissenting Essays in American
    History*. New York: Pantheon Books, 1968.
Stromberg, Roland. "American Business and the Approach of War, 1935–
    1941." *Journal of Economic History* 13 (Winter 1953): 58–78.
Toscano, Mario. "Eden's Mission to Rome on the Eve of the Italo-Ethiopian
    Conflict." In Sarkissian, ed., *Studies in Diplomatic History and
    Historiography in Honour of G. P. Gooch, C.H.* London: Longmans,
    1961.
Trefousse, H. L. "Failure of German Intelligence in the United States, 1935–
    1945." *Mississippi Valley Historical Review* 42 (June 1955): 84–100.
Valaik, David J. "Catholics, Neutrality, and the Spanish Embargo, 1937–1939."
    Journal of American History 54 (June 1967): 73–85.
Vaudagna, Maurizio. "The New Deal and Corporatism in Italy." *Radical
    History Review* 4 (Spring–Summer 1977): 3–35.
Vieth, Jane Karoline. "Joseph P. Kennedy and British Appeasement: The
    Diplomacy of a Boston Irishman." In Kenneth P. Jones, ed., *U.S.
    Diplomats in Europe, 1919–1941*. Santa Barbara, Calif.: ABC-Clio,
    1981.
————. "Munich Revisited through Joseph P. Kennedy's Eyes."*Michigan
    Academician* 18, no. 1 (Winter 1986): 73–85.
Wallace, William. "Roosevelt and British Appeasement in 1938." *Bulletin
    British Association for American Studies* 5 (1962): 4–30.
Watt, D. C. "The German Diplomats and the Nazi Leaders, 1933–1939."
    Journal of Central European Affairs 15 (July 1955): 148–60.
————. "The Anglo-German Naval Agreement of 1935: An Interim Judg-
    ment." *Journal of Modern History* 28 (June 1956): 155–75.
————. "The Rome-Berlin Axis, 1936–1940: Myth and Reality." *Review of
    Politics* (October 1960): 519–43.
————. "The Secret Laval-Mussolini Agreement on Ethiopia." *Middle East
    Journal* 15 (Winter 1961): 69–78.
————. "Roosevelt and Chamberlain: Two Appeasers."*International Journal*
    28, no. 1 (1972–73): 185–204.
Webster, Charles. "Munich Reconsidered: A Survey of British Policy." *Inter-
    national Affairs* 37 (April 1961): 137–53.
Weinberg, Gerhard. "The May Crisis, 1938." *Journal of Modern History* 29
    (September 1957): 213–25.
————. "Hitler's Image of the United States." *American Historical Review* 69
    (July 1964): 1006–21.

Wiltz, John E. "The Nye Committee Revisited." *The Historian* 23 (February 1961): 211-33.

Books

Alexander, Bill. *British Volunteers for Liberty: Spain 1936-1939.* London: Lawrence and Wishart, 1982.

Alsop, Joseph and Robert Kintner. *American White Paper: The Story of American Diplomacy and the Second World War.* New York: Random House, 1940.

Baer, George W. *Test Case: Italy, Ethiopia, and the League of Nations.* Stanford, Calif.: Hoover Institution Press, 1976.

Barnes, Harry Elmer, ed. *Perpetual War for Perpetual Peace: A Critical Examination of the Foreign Policy of Franklin Delano Roosevelt and Its Aftermath.* Caldwell, Idaho: Caxton Printers, 1953.

Beard, Charles. *American Foreign Policy in the Making, 1932-1940: A Study in Responsibilities.* New Haven, Conn.: Yale University Press, 1946.

————. *President Roosevelt and the Coming of the War, 1941.* New Haven, Conn.: Yale University Press, 1948.

Beckett, Grace. *The Reciprocal Trade Agreements Program.* New York: Columbia University Press, 1951.

Bendiner, Robert. *The Riddle of the State Department.* New York: Farrar, 1942.

Beschloss, Michael R. *Kennedy and Roosevelt: The Uneasy Alliance.* New York: W. W. Norton, 1980.

Borg, Dorothy. *The United States and the Far Eastern Crisis, 1933-1938: From the Manchurian Incident Through the Initial Stage of the Undeclared Sino-Japanese War.* Cambridge, Mass.: Harvard University Press, 1964.

Brook-Shepherd, Gordon. *The Anschluss.* Philadelphia: Lippincott, 1963.

Bullock, Alan. *Hitler: A Study in Tyranny.* Rev. ed., New York: Harper & Row, 1962.

Burns, James MacGregor. *Roosevelt: The Lion and the Fox.* New York: Harcourt, Brace, and World, 1956.

Carlton, David. *Anthony Eden: A Biography.* London: Allen Lane, 1981.

Cassels, Alan. *Mussolini's Early Diplomacy.* Princeton, N.J.: Princeton University Press, 1970.

————. *Fascist Italy.* Second ed., Arlington Heights, Ill.: Harlan Davidson, 1985.

Cattell, David T. *Soviet Diplomacy and the Spanish Civil War.* Berkeley: University of California Press, 1957.

Churchill, Winston S. *The Gathering Storm.* New York: Bantam Books, 1961.

Cole, Wayne S. *Senator Gerald P. Nye and American Foreign Relations.* Minneapolis: University of Minnesota Press, 1962.

————. *An Interpretive History of American Foreign Relations.* Homewood, Ill.: Dorsey Press, 1968.

————. *Roosevelt and the Isolationists, 1932–45.* Lincoln: University of Nebraska Press, 1983.

Colvin, Ian. *The Chamberlain Cabinet: How the Meetings in 10 Downing Street, 1937–1939, Led to the Second World War.* London: Gollancz, 1971.

Compton, James W. *The Swastika and the Eagle: Hitler, the United States, and the Origins of World War II.* Boston: Houghton Mifflin, 1967.

Crane, Katharine. *Mr. Carr of State: Forty-Seven Years in the Department of State.* New York: St. Martin's Press, 1960.

Current, Richard N. *Secretary Stimson: A Study in Statecraft.* New Brunswick, N.J.: Rutgers University Press, 1954.

Dallek, Robert. *Democrat and Diplomat: The Life of William E. Dodd.* New York: Oxford University Press, 1968.

————. *Franklin D. Roosevelt and American Foreign Policy, 1932–1945.* New York: Oxford University Press, 1979.

De Conde, Alexander. *Half Bitter, Half Sweet: An Excursion into Italian-American History.* New York: Charles Scribner's Sons, 1971.

Delzell, Charles F. *Mussolini's Enemies: The Italian Anti-Fascist Resistance.* Princeton, N.J.: Princeton University Press, 1961.

DeSantis, Hugh. *The Diplomacy of Silence.* Chicago: University of Chicago Press, 1983.

Diggins, John P. *Mussolini and Fascism: The View from America.* Princeton, N.J.: Princeton University Press, 1972.

Dilks, David, ed. *Diaries of Sir Alexander Cadogan, 1938–1945.* New York: Putnam, 1971.

Divine, Robert A., ed. *The Illusion of Neutrality: Franklin D. Roosevelt and the Struggle Over the Arms Embargo.* Chicago: University of Chicago Press, 1962.

————. *Causes and Consequences of World War II.* Chicago: Quadrangle Books, 1969.

————. *Roosevelt and World War II.* Baltimore: Johns Hopkins Press, 1969.

————. *The Reluctant Belligerent: American Entry into World War II.* New York: Wiley, 1979.

Drummond, Donald F. *The Passing of American Neutrality, 1937–1941.* Ann Arbor: University of Michigan Press, 1955.

Eden, Anthony. *Facing the Dictators.* Boston: Houghton Mifflin, 1962.

Edwards, Jill. *The British Government and the Spanish Civil War 1936–1939.* New York: Macmillan, 1979.

Eubank, Keith. *Munich.* Norman: University of Oklahoma Press, 1963.

Everest, Allen S. *Morgenthau, the New Deal, and Silver.* New York: King's Crown Press, 1950.

Farnsworth, Beatrice. *William C. Bullitt and the Soviet Union*. Bloomington: Indiana University Press, 1967.

Feiling, Keith. *The Life of Neville Chamberlain*. London: Macmillan, 1946.

Feis, Herbert. *Seen From E. A.: Three International Episodes*. New York: Knopf, 1947.

————. *The Diplomacy of the Dollar: First Era 1919–1932*. Baltimore: Johns Hopkins Press, 1950.

————. *The Road to Pearl Harbor: The Coming of the War Between the United States and Japan*. Princeton, N.J.: Princeton University Press, 1950.

Freidel, Frank. *Franklin D. Roosevelt: Apprenticeship*. Boston: Little, Brown, 1952.

————. *Franklin D. Roosevelt: Ordeal*. Boston: Little, Brown, 1954.

————. *Franklin D. Roosevelt: Triumph*. Boston: Little Brown, 1956.

————. *F.D.R.: Launching the New Deal*. Boston: Little, Brown, 1973.

Friedlander, Saul. *Hitler et les Etats-Unis (1939–1941)*. Geneva: Librairie Droz, 1963.

Frye, Alton. *Nazi Germany and the American Hemisphere, 1933–1941*. New Haven, Conn.: Yale University Press, 1967.

Furnia, Arthur H. *The Diplomacy of Appeasement: Anglo-French Relations and the Prelude to World War II, 1931–1938*. Washington, D.C.: University Press of Washington D.C., 1960.

Gardner, Lloyd. *Economic Aspects of New Deal Diplomacy*. Madison: University of Wisconsin Press, 1964.

George, Margaret. *The Warped Vision: British Foreign Policy, 1933–1938*. Pittsburgh: University of Pittsburgh Press, 1965.

Gilbert, Martin and Richard Gott. *The Appeasers*. Boston: Houghton Mifflin, 1963.

Goodwin, Doris Kearns. *The Fitzgeralds and the Kennedys: An American Saga*. New York: Simon and Schuster, 1987.

Graff, Frank Warren. *The Strategy of Involvement: A Diplomatic Biography of Sumner Welles, 1933–1943*. New York: Garland, 1988.

Gunther, John. *Roosevelt in Retrospect: A Profile in History*. New York: Harper, 1950.

Guttmann, Allen. *The Sound in the Heart: America and the Spanish Civil War*. New York: Free Press, 1962.

Harris, Brice, Jr. *The United States and the Italo-Ethiopian Crisis*. Stanford, Calif.: Stanford University Press, 1964.

Hearden, Patrick. *Roosevelt Confronts Hitler: America's Entry into World War II*. DeKalb: Northern Illinois University Press, 1987.

Heiden, Konrad. *Der Fuehrer: Hitler's Rise to Power*. Boston: Houghton Mifflin, 1944.

Hilberg, Raul. *The Destruction of the European Jews*. Rev. ed., Chicago: Quadrangle Books, 1961.

154   Selected Bibliography

Hunt, Michael H. *Ideology and U.S. Foreign Policy*. New Haven, Conn.: Yale
    University Press, 1987.
Israel, Fred. *Nevada's Key Pittman*. Lincoln: University of Nebraska Press,
    1963.
Jablon, Howard. *Crossroads of Decision: The State Department and Foreign
    Policy, 1933–1937*. Lexington: University of Kentucky Press, 1983.
Jackson, Gabriel. *The Spanish Republic and the Civil War 1931–1939*.
    Princeton, N.J.: Princeton University Press, 1965.
Jarman, Thomas L. *The Rise and Fall of Nazi Germany*. New York: New York
    University Press, 1956.
Jonas, Manfred. *Isolationism in America, 1935–1941*. Ithaca, N.Y.: Cornell
    University Press, 1966.
Jones, Kenneth Paul, ed. *US Diplomats in Europe, 1919–1941*. Santa Barbara,
    Calif.: ABC-Clio, 1981.
Kanawada, Leo V., Jr. *Franklin D. Roosevelt's Diplomacy and American
    Catholics, Italians, and Jews*. Ann Arbor, Mich.: UMI Research Press,
    1982.
Kennan, George F. *American Diplomacy, 1900–1950*. Chicago: University of
    Chicago Press, 1951.
Kimball, Warren. *Franklin D. Roosevelt and the World Crisis, 1937–1945*.
    Lexington, Mass.: D. C. Heath, 1973.
Kleine-Ahlbrandt, W. Laird. *The Policy of Simmering: A Study of British Policy
    During the Spanish Civil War, 1936–1939*. The Hague: M. Nijhoff, 1962.
———, ed. *Appeasement of the Dictators*. New York: Holt, Rinehart and
    Winston, 1970.
Koliopoulos, John S. *Greece and the British Connection 1935–1941*. New York:
    Clarendon Press, 1977.
Laffan, R. G. D. *The Crisis over Czechoslovakia, January to September, 1938*.
    Oxford: Oxford University Press, 1951.
Langer, William L. and S. Everett Gleason. *The Challenge to Isolation: The
    World Crisis of 1937–1940 and American Foreign Policy*. 2 vols. New
    York: Harper and Row, 1964.
———. *The Undeclared War, 1940–1941*. New York: Harper and Row, 1953.
Lee, Bradford A. *Britain and the Sino-Japanese War, 1937–1939: A Study in
    the Dilemmas of British Decline*. Stanford, Calif.: Stanford University
    Press, 1973.
Leith-Ross, Frederick. *Money Talks: Fifty Years of International Finance*.
    London: Hutchinson, 1968.
Leuchtenburg, William E. *Franklin D. Roosevelt and the New Deal, 1932–1940*.
    New York: Harper and Row, 1963.
Liggio, Leonard P., and James J. Martin, eds. *Watershed to Empire: Essays on
    New Deal Foreign Policy*. Colorado Springs, Col.: R. Myles, 1976.

Little, Douglas. *Malevolent Neutrality: The United States, Great Britain, and the Origins of the Spanish Civil War*. Ithaca, N.Y.: Cornell University Press, 1985.

Louis, William Roger. *British Strategy in the Far East, 1919–1939*. Oxford: Clarendon Press, 1971.

Lyttelton, Adrian. *The Seizure of Power: Fascism in Italy, 1919–1929*. New York: Charles Scribner's Sons, 1973.

McKenna, Marian. *Borah*. Ann Arbor: University of Michigan Press, 1961.

MacDonald, C. A. *The United States, Britain and Appeasement, 1936–1939*. New York: St. Martin's Press, 1981.

Mack Smith, Denis. *Mussolini*. New York: Knopf, 1982.

Macleod, Iain. *Neville Chamberlain*. New York: Atheneum, 1961.

Maddux, Thomas R. *Years of Estrangement: American Relations with the Soviet Union, 1933–1941*. Tallahassee: University Presses of Florida, 1980.

Maier, Charles. *Recasting Bourgeois Europe*. Princeton, N.J.: Princeton University Press, 1975.

Marks, Frederick W. *Wind Over Sand: The Diplomacy of Franklin Roosevelt*. Athens: University of Georgia Press, 1988.

Middlemas, Keith. *The Strategy of Appeasement*. Chicago: Quadrangle Books, 1972.

Migone, Gian Giacomo. *Problemi di storia nei rapporti tra Italia e Stati Uniti*. Torino: Rosenberg and Sellier, 1971.

Mommsen, Wolfgang J. and Lothar Kettenacker, eds. *The Fascist Challenge and the Policy of Appeasement*. London: George Allen & Unwin, 1983.

Morison, Etling E. *Turmoil and Tradition: A Study of the Life and Times of Henry L. Stimson*. Boston: Houghton Mifflin, 1960.

Morse, Arthur D. *While Six Million Died: A Chronicle of American Apathy*. New York: Random House, 1968.

Namier, Lewis B. *Diplomatic Prelude, 1938–1939*. London: H. Fertig, 1948.

Nevins, Allan. *The New Deal and World Affairs: A Chronicle of International Affairs, 1933–1945*. New Haven, Conn.: Yale University Press, 1945.

Northedge, F. S. *The Troubled Giant*. London: G. Bell & Sons, 1966.

Offner, Arnold A. *American Appeasement: United States Foreign Policy and Germany, 1933–1938*. New York: W. W. Norton, 1969.

———. *Origins of the Second World War: American Foreign Policy and World Politics, 1917–1941*. New York: Praeger, 1975.

Ovendale, Ritchie. *"Appeasement" and the English Speaking World*. Cardiff: University of Wales Press, 1975.

Pratt, Julius W. *Cordell Hull*. 2 vols. New York: Cooper Square Publishers, 1964.

Puzzo, Dante. *Spain and the Great Powers 1936–1941*. New York: Columbia University Press, 1962.

Range, Willard. *Franklin D. Roosevelt's World Order*. Athens: University of
     Georgia Press, 1959.
Rauch, Basil. *Roosevelt: From Munich to Pearl Harbor*. New York: Creative
     Age Press, 1950.
Reynolds, David. *The Creation of the Anglo-American Alliance 1937–1941*.
     Chapel Hill: University of North Carolina Press, 1982.
Robertson, E. M. *Hitler's Pre-War Policy and Military Plans, 1933–1939*.
     London: Citadel Press, 1963.
Rock, William R. *Appeasement on Trial: British Foreign Policy and Its Critics,
     1938–1939*. Hamden, Conn.: Archon Books, 1966.
Rose, Norman. *Vansittart: Study of a Diplomat*. New York: Holmes and Meier,
     1978.
Rothfels, Hans. *The German Opposition to Hitler: An Appraisal*. Hinsdale, Ill.:
     H. Regnery, 1948.
Rothstein, Andrew. *The Munich Conspiracy*. London: Lawrence and Wishart,
     1958.
Rowse, A. L. *Appeasement: A Study in Political Decline, 1933–39*. New York:
     Norton, 1961.
Ruddy, T. Michael. *The Cautious Diplomat: Charles E. Bohlen and the Soviet
     Union, 1929–1969*. Kent, Ohio: Kent State University Press, 1986.
Salvermini, Gaetano. *Under the Axe of Fascism*. New York: Viking Press, 1936.
———. *The Origins of Fascism in Italy*. New York: Harper and Row, 1973.
Schlesinger, Arthur M., Jr. *The Coming of the New Deal*. Boston: Houghton
     Mifflin, 1959.
Schmitz, David F. *The United States and Fascist Italy, 1922–1940*. Chapel Hill:
     University of North Carolina Press, 1988.
Schröder, Hans-Jurgen. *Deutschland und die Vereinigten Staaten 1933–1939*.
     Weisbaden, West Germany: F. Steiner, 1970.
Schulzinger, Robert D. *The Making of the Diplomatic Mind: The Training,
     Outlook, and Style of United States Foreign Service Officers, 1908–
     1931*. Middletown, Conn.: Wesleyan University Press, 1975.
Schwarz, Jordon A. *Liberal: Adolf A. Berle and the Vision of an American Era*.
     New York: Free Press, 1987.
Seabury, Paul. *The Wilhelmstrasse: A Study of German Diplomats Under the
     Nazi Regime*. Berkeley: University of California Press, 1954.
Seldes, George. *Sawdust Caesar*. New York: Harper and Brothers, 1935.
Seton-Watson, Christopher. *Italy From Liberalism to Fascism, 1870–1925*.
     London: Methuen, 1967.
Sherwood, Robert E. *Roosevelt and Hopkins: An Intimate History*. New York:
     Harper and Brothers, 1948.
Shirer, William L. *The Rise and Fall of the Third Reich: A History of Nazi
     Germany*. New York: Simon and Schuster, 1960.
Smith, Janet Adam. *John Buchan*. London: Oxford University Press, 1965.

Spini, Giorgio, G. G. Migone, and Massimo Teodori, eds. *Italia e America dalla Grande Guerra a oggi.* Venice: Marsilio, 1976.

Steel, Ronald. *Walter Lippman and the American Century.* New York: Vintage, 1980.

Stiller, Jesse H. *George S. Messersmith: Diplomat of Democracy.* Chapel Hill: University of North Carolina Press, 1987.

Stromberg, Roland N. *Collective Security and American Foreign Policy: From the League of Nations to NATO.* New York: Praeger, 1963.

Stuart, Graham H. *The Department of State: A History of Its Organization, Procedure, and Personnel.* New York: Macmillan, 1949.

Taylor, A. J. P. *The Course of German History: A Survey of the Development of German History Since 1815.* London: Coward–McCann, 1945.

————. *Origins of the Second World War.* New York: Atheneum, 1962.

————. *English History, 1914–1945.* New York: Oxford University Press, 1965.

Taylor, F. Jay. *The United States and the Spanish Civil War.* New York: Bookman Associates, 1956.

Taylor, Telford. *Munich.* New York: Doubleday, 1979.

Thomas, Hugh. *The Spanish Civil War.* New York: Harper and Row, 1977.

Torina, Richard P. *American Diplomacy and the Spanish Civil War.* Bloomington: Indiana University Press, 1968.

Trefousse, H. L. *Germany and American Neutrality, 1939–1941.* New York: Bookman Associates, 1951.

Tugwell, Rexford Guy. *The Democratic Roosevelt: A Biography of Franklin D. Roosevelt.* New York: Doubleday, 1957.

Watkins, K. W. *Britain Divided: The Effect of the Spanish Civil War on British Political Opinion.* London: Nelson, 1963.

Watt, D. C. *Too Serious a Business: European Armed Forces and the Approach to the Second World War.* Berkeley: University of California Press, 1975.

Weil, Martin. *A Pretty Good Club: The Founding Fathers of the United States Foreign Service.* New York: Norton, 1978.

Weinberg, Gerhard L. *The Foreign Policy of Hitler's Germany.* Chicago: University of Chicago Press, 1972.

Whalen, Richard J. *The Founding Father: The Story of Joseph P. Kennedy.* New York: New American Library, 1964.

Wheeler-Bennett, John W. *Munich: Prologue to Tragedy.* New York: Duell, Sloan & Pearce, 1948.

————. *The Nemesis of Power: The German Army in Politics, 1918–1945.* New York: Macmillan, 1964.

————. *The Pipe Dream of Peace: The Story of the Collapse of Disarmament.* New York: William Morrow, 1971.

Wilkins, Mira. *The Maturing of the Multinational Enterprise.* Cambridge, Mass.: Harvard University Press, 1974.

Williams, William A. *The Tragedy of American Diplomacy.* 2nd revised ed., New York: Dell, 1972.

Wiltz, John E. *From Isolation to War, 1931–1941.* New York: Crowell, 1968.

Wiskemann, Elizabeth. *The Rome–Berlin Axis: A Study of the Relations Between Hitler and Mussolini.* Rev. ed., London: Collins, 1966.

Wood, Bryce. *The Making of the Good Neighbor Policy.* New York: Columbia University Press, 1961.

Wyman, David. *Paper Walls: America and the Refugee Crisis, 1938–1941.* Amherst: University of Massachusetts Press, 1968.

Unpublished Material

Bauer, Wolfred. "The Shipment of American Strategic Raw Materials to Nazi Germany: A Study in United States Economic Foreign Policy, 1933–1939." Ph.D. dissertation, University of Washington, 1964.

Burke, Bernard Vincent. "American Diplomats and Hitler's Rise to Power, 1930–1933: The Mission of Ambassador Sackett." Ph.D. dissertation, University of Washington, 1966.

Buzzell, Rolfe G. "The Eagle and the Fasces: The United States and Italy, 1935–1939." Ph.D. dissertation, University of California, Santa Barbara, 1977.

De Santi, Louis A. "United States Relations with Italy Under Mussolini, 1922–1940." Ph.D. dissertation, Columbia University, 1951.

Ehlers, Caroline Keith. "William Phillips: The Failure of a Mission." M.A. thesis, University of Maryland, 1979.

Harrison, Richard A. "Appeasement and Isolation: The Relationship of British and American Foreign Policies, 1935–1938." Ph.D. dissertation, Princeton University, 1974.

Irvin, Thomas C. "Norman H. Davis and the Quest for Arms Control, 1927–1937." Ph.D. dissertation, Ohio State University, 1963.

Jordan, Laylon W. "America's Mussolini: The United States and Italy, 1919–1936." Ph.D. dissertation, University of Virginia, 1972.

Millsap, Mary P. "Mussolini and the United States: Italo-American Relations, 1935–1941." Ph.D. dissertation, University of California, Los Angeles, 1972.

Moss, Kenneth. "Bureaucrat as Diplomat: George S. Messersmith and the State Department Approach to War, 1933–1941." Ph.D. dissertation, University of Minnesota, 1978.

Remak, Joachim. "Germany and the United States, 1933–1939." Ph.D. dissertation, Stanford University, 1956.

Tudor, Mary Jo. "President Roosevelt's Peace Moves in Europe, September, 1937 to May, 1939." M.A. thesis, University of Maryland, 1967.

Whitehead, Donald F. "The Making of Foreign Policy During President Roosevelt's First Term, 1933–1937." Ph.D. dissertation, University of Chicago, 1951.

Index

Cuse, Robert, 28
Czech crisis, 51–52, 54–71

Daladier, Edward, 18, 67
Dalton, Hugh, 32
Davis, Norman H., 114, 115, 130
de Bianchi, Jose Antonio, 30
del Vayo, Julio Alvarez, 39
Dodd, William E., 7, 139 n.71
Dunn, James Clement, xix, xxi, 25,
85, 91; views on the Spanish
Civil War, 30, 36, 43

Easter Pact, 126
Eden, Anthony, 25, 34, 96, 113,
116, 123, 130; fear of bolshevism, xx, 23, 24, 27; questioning
of Britain's policies, 21, 31–32,
35, 44, 125; resignation of, 35,
126
Einstein, Albert, 29
Engert, C. Van H., 87
Ethiopia. See Italo-Ethiopian war

Farley, James, 40
Fascism. See United States, view
of fascism
Fisher, Warren, 113
France, 14–16, 34, 55, 85
Franco, Francisco, 25, 42. See also
Spanish Civil War

Geneva Disarmament Conference,
117–18
Germany, 92; and the Spanish
Civil War, 14–15, 27, 33. See
also Anschluss; Czech crisis;
Hitler, Adolf
Great Britain: appeasement policy
of, xiv, xv, xix, 51–52; fear of
bolshevism, 22, 23, 26; and the
Spanish Civil War, 14–16, 21,
26, 27, 31; view of Japan, 128–

29; view of United States, 103–
4, 106, 110–11, 118; war debts
owed to United States, 108–11.
See also Chamberlain, Neville;
specific British government officials
Greek Popular Front, 23
Green, Joseph, 46 n.23

Hackworth, Green, 38
Halifax, Lord (Edward Frederick
Lindley Wood), 26–27, 35–37,
42, 56
Henlein, Konrad, 56
Hitler, Adolf, 52, 82, 117, 119. See
also Anschluss; Czech crisis;
Roosevelt, Franklin Delano,
view of Hitler; United States,
view of Hitler
Hoare, Samuel, 31, 33, 34, 115
Hoare-Laval plan, 10, 88, 120
Hoover, J. Edgar, 28
Hopkins, Harry, 87
Hull, Cordell, 18, 84, 86–88, 89,
91, 106–7, 114, 136 n.42; and
the Czech crisis, 56, 62–63; op-
position to peace conference, 94,
125; and the Spanish Civil War,
26, 30, 37, 38, 40, 43

Ickes, Harold, 30, 38, 57, 64
International Brigades, 28
Italo-Ethiopian war, 11–12, 75–77,
79–81, 84, 87–88
Italy, 82, 91–92; and the Spanish
Civil War, 14–15, 27–28, 33, 89–
91. See also Italo-Ethiopian war;
Mussolini
ITT (International Telephone and
Telegraph), 22, 24, 29, 37, 43

Japan, 117, 129, 130. See also Roo-

sevelt, Franklin Delano; United
States
Johnson Act, 110

Kellogg-Briand Pact, 86
Kennedy, Joseph P., xx, 8, 17, 53–
54, 56–70
Krock, Arthur, 29, 40, 49 n.66

Lausanne formula, 109
League of Nations, 12, 35, 55, 76–
78, 86, 119–20
Leith-Ross, Frederick, 111
Lerner, Max, 38
Lindsay, Ronald, 108, 110, 113,
126–27, 131
Locarno Agreement, 55
London Economic Conference, xx
Long, Breckinridge, 12–13, 23, 24,
39, 81–85, 88

MacDonald, J. Ramsay, 110, 112
MacDonald's disarmament plan,
117, 127
MacVeagh, Lincoln, 23
Masarky, Jan, 68
Messersmith, George, xxi
Metaxas, Ioannis, 23
Moffat, Pierrepont, xix, xxi, 23, 36,
85; support of Franco, 37–38,
42–44
Moore, Walter, 28
Morgan, John H., 46 n.23
Morgenthau, Henry, Jr., 30, 38, 63,
112, 113–14, 123
Munich Pact, xx, 17–18, 51, 52,
68–70. See also Czech crisis
Mussolini, Benito, 68, 81, 92–93,
97; and Ethiopia, 23, 84, 87. See
also Italo-Ethiopian war; Italy;
United States, view of Mussolini

Naval Treaty of 1936, 129

Negrin, Juan, 39, 43
Neutrality Act, 11–12, 30–31, 38,
41, 76–77, 87–88, 119
NIC (Non-Intervention Commit-
tee), 14, 34, 37, 120
Nicolson, Harold, 33
Nine-Power Treaty, 127
Nye, Gerald, 40
Nye Resolution, 40
Nyon Agreement, 33–34

O'Mally, Owen, 42
Open Door Policy, xvi–xvii, 99
n.15
Ormsby-Gore, William, 34

Pearson, Drew, 38
Perkins, Mahlon, 32
Phillips, William, xix, 10, 12–13,
24–26, 29–30; and Italy, 31, 85,
89, 91; view of Mussolini, 82,
90–91, 96
Pittman, Key, 40
Poland, 52, 71

Reciprocal Trade Agreement, xvi
Roosevelt, Franklin Delano: and
Anglo-American trade, 114,
116; attitude toward appeasement and isolationist policies,
xvi, xix–xx, 4, 13, 18, 36, 53;
and Canada, 63, 123, 125, 131;
and the Czech crisis, 66–67, 70;
diplomatic style of, 108, 111,
122, 133 n.2; doubts about nonintervention, 21, 44; and Germany, 29–30, 118–19; and the
Italo-Ethiopian war, 75–76, 87,
92, 95–96; and Kennedy, 8, 9,
64–65; and the Neutrality Act,
11, 87, 119–20, 124, 130–31;
non-commitment to Britain of,
63–64, 66, 105; peace plans, 93–

About the Editors and Contributors

RICHARD D. CHALLENER is Professor of History at Princeton University and the author of many books, including *Admirals, Generals, and American Foreign Policy, 1898–1914.*

WAYNE S. COLE is Professor of History at the University of Maryland and is the author of many books on American foreign policy. His most recent is *Norway and the United States, 1905–1955: Two Democracies in Peace and War.*

RICHARD A. HARRISON is Associate Professor of History at Pomona College in Claremont, California. He has written numerous articles that have appeared in *Diplomatic History, The Canadian Journal of History/Annales Canadiennes d'Histoires, International History Review,* and *Pacific Historical Review.*

DOUGLAS LITTLE is Associate Professor of History at Clark University in Worcester, Massachusetts. He has written numerous articles and books and is currently doing research on the United States's relationship with the Middle East from 1945 to 1967.

DAVID F. SCHMITZ is Associate Professor of History at Whitman College in Walla Walla, Washington, and is the author of *The United States and Fascist Italy*.

JANE KAROLINE VIETH is Professor of History at Michigan State University. She has written several articles and has contributed to *U.S. Diplomats in Europe (1919–1941)* (Kenneth Paul Jones, ed.) and *Modern American Diplomacy* (John M. Carroll and George C. Herring, eds.).